RUTHERFORD & SON

by Githa Sowerby

SAMUEL FRENCH

samuelfrench.co.uk

Copyright © 1924 by Githa Sowerby
All Rights Reserved

RUTHERFORD & SON is fully protected under the copyright laws of the British Commonwealth, including Canada, the United States of America, and all other countries of the Copyright Union. All rights, including professional and amateur stage productions, recitation, lecturing, public reading, motion picture, radio broadcasting, television and the rights of translation into foreign languages are strictly reserved.

ISBN 978-0-573-11520-2

www.samuelfrench.co.uk
www.samuelfrench.com

For Amateur Production Enquiries

UNITED KINGDOM AND WORLD
EXCLUDING NORTH AMERICA
plays@samuelfrench.co.uk
020 7255 4302/01

Each title is subject to availability from Samuel French, depending upon country of performance.

CAUTION: Professional and amateur producers are hereby warned that RUTHERFORD & SON is subject to a licensing fee. Publication of this play does not imply availability for performance. Both amateurs and professionals considering a production are strongly advised to apply to the appropriate agent before starting rehearsals, advertising, or booking a theatre. A licensing fee must be paid whether the title is presented for charity or gain and whether or not admission is charged.

The Professional Rights in this play are controlled by Samuel French Ltd, 24-32 Stephenson Way, London NW1 2HD.

No one shall make any changes in this title for the purpose of production. No part of this book may be reproduced, stored in a retrieval system, or transmitted in any form, by any means, now known or yet to be invented, including mechanical, electronic, photocopying, recording, videotaping, or otherwise, without the prior written permission of the publisher. No one shall upload this title, or part of this title, to any social media websites.

The right of Githa Sowerby to be identified as author of this work has been asserted in accordance with Section 77 of the Copyright, Designs and Patents Act 1988.

THINKING ABOUT PERFORMING A SHOW?

There are thousands of plays and musicals available to perform from Samuel French right now, and applying for a licence is easier and more affordable than you might think

From classic plays to brand new musicals, from monologues to epic dramas, there are shows for everyone.

Plays and musicals are protected by copyright law so if you want to perform them, the first thing you'll need is a licence. This simple process helps support the playwright by ensuring they get paid for their work, and means that you'll have the documents you need to stage the show in public.

Not all our shows are available to perform all the time, so it's important to check and apply for a licence before you start rehearsals or commit to doing the show.

LEARN MORE & FIND THOUSANDS OF SHOWS

Browse our full range of plays and musicals and find out more about how to license a show

www.samuelfrench.co.uk/perform

Talk to the friendly experts in our Licensing team for advice on choosing a show, and help with licensing

plays@samuelfrench.co.uk   020 7387 9373

Acting Editions
BORN TO PERFORM

Playscripts designed from the ground up to work the way you do in rehearsal, performance and study

---

Larger, clearer text for easier reading

Wider margins for notes

Performance features such as character and props lists, sound and lighting cues, and more

---

+ CHOOSE A SIZE AND STYLE TO SUIT YOU

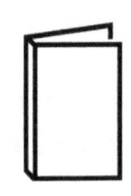

STANDARD EDITION
Our regular paperback book at our regular size

SPIRAL-BOUND EDITION
The same size as the Standard Edition, but with a sturdy, easy-to-fold, easy-to-hold spiral-bound spine

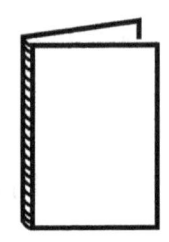

LARGE EDITION
A4 size and spiral bound, with larger text and a blank page for notes opposite every page of text. Perfect for technical and directing use

---

| LEARN MORE | samuelfrench.co.uk/actingeditions

**Other plays by GITHA SOWERBY
published and licensed by Samuel French**

A Man and Some Women

Before Breakfast

Direct Action

Sheila

The Policeman's Whistle

The Stepmother

**FIND PERFECT PLAYS TO PERFORM AT
www.samuelfrench.co.uk/perform**

ABOUT THE AUTHOR

Katherine Githa Sowerby was born in 1876 in Gateshead, England. Her first play, *Rutherford & Son*, was an outstanding success when originally performed in 1912. Published under her initials G.K. Sowerby, it was generally assumed that the author was a man. When her true identity was revealed she became an overnight sensation. *Rutherford & Son* ran for one hundred and thirty-three performances in London and sixty-three performances in New York and was translated into numerous languages. Other plays followed: *Before Breakfast*, 1912; *A Man and Some Women*, 1914; *Sheila*, in 1917; *The Stepmother*, 1924; and finally, *The Policeman's Whistle*, 1934. She was well-known in the early twentieth century as a feminist and voice of the people, but she by the time of her death in 1970, she and her works had lapsed into obscurity.

Rutherford & Son was revived in 1980 and there have been numerous productions since.

Rutherford & Son was first perfomed at the Court Theatre, London, on 31st January 1912, with the following cast:

ANN	Agnes Thomas
MARY	Thyrza Norman
JANET	Edyth Olive
JOHN	Edmund Breon
RICHARD	Frank Randell
JOHN RUTHERFORD	Norman McKinnel
MARTIN	A.S. Homewood
MRS HENDERSON	Agnes Hill

Produced by John Leigh

Rutherford & Son was revived at the Royal National Theatre in May 1994, with the following cast:

ANN	June Watson
MARY	Phoebe Nicolls
JANET	Brid Brennan
JOHN	Sean Chapman
RICHARD	Wayne Foskett
JOHN RUTHERFORD	Bob Peck
MARTIN	Tom Mannion
MRS HENDERSON	Jenny Howe

Directed by Katie Mitchell

CHARACTERS

ANN
MARY
JANET
JOHN
RICHARD
JOHN RUTHERFORD
MARTIN
MRS HENDERSON

ACT ONE

SCENE: *living room in* **JOHN RUTHERFORD**'s *house.*

Two days elapse between Acts One and Two. One night between Acts Two and Three.

JOHN RUTHERFORD's *house stands on the edge of the moor, far enough from the village to serve its dignity and near enough to admit of the master going to and from the Works in a few minutes – a process known to the household as 'going across'. The living room, in which the family life has centred for generations, is a big square room furnished in solid mahogany and papered in red, as if to mitigate the bleakness of a climate that includes five months of winter in every year. There is a big table in the middle of the room covered with a brown cloth at which the family take their meals. An air of orderliness pervades the room, which perhaps accounts for its being extremely uncomfortable. From above the heavy polished sideboard the late* **JOHN RUTHERFORD** *looks down from his frame and sees the settle and armchair on either side of the fire, the marble clock on the mantelpiece, the desk with its brass inkstand and neatly arranged bundles of papers precisely as he saw them in life.*

On this particular evening in December **ANN RUTHERFORD** *is sitting by the fire alternately knitting and dozing. She is a faded, querulous woman of about sixty, and wears a black dress with a big flat brooch and a cap with lilac ribbons.* **MARY RUTHERFORD**, *a gentle delicate-looking woman of twenty-six, is seated on the settle opposite to her making a baby's cap; she is bending forward to catch the light of the fire on her work, for the lamp has not yet been brought in.*

Presently JANET *comes in carrying a silver basket and a pair of carpet slippers. She is a heavy, dark woman, some ten years older than* MARY, *with an expressionless tired face and monotonous voice. All her movements are slipshod and aimless, and she seldom raises her eyes. She is dressed in a dark dress of some warm material with white collar and cuffs.*

JANET *(glancing at the clock)* He's not back yet.

ANN No... If you mean your father.

JANET *(folding up the brown cloth preparatory to laying the table)* Who else should I mean?

ANN You might mean any one... You always talk about he and him, as if there was no one else in the house.

JANET There isn't.

ANN Answer me back, that's the way. (JANET *makes no reply. She puts the silver basket on the table and comes to the fire with the slippers)* There – put his slippers down to warm. The Committee room's cold as ice, and he'll come in like the dead.

MARY *(looking up from her work for a moment)* I believe it's going to freeze tonight – the furnaces are flaring so.

JANET *drops the shoes one by one on to the hearthrug without stooping.*

ANN They'll never warm there! I never seed sic a feckless lass. *(Stoops laboriously and sets them up against the fender)* Is the dinner all right?

JANET Susan's let the pie get burnt, but I've scraped the top off – he won't notice. The girdle cake's as tough as leather. She'll have to do a fresh one – if there's time.

ANN You might ha' seen to things a bit.

JANET I have. There wouldn't ha' been a pie at all if I hadn't. The oven damper's gone wrong.

ANN Answer me – answer yer aunt! You and your dampers – and there you are a-laying the table and ye know weel enough yer father's forbid you to do things like a servant.

JANET What else is there to do? I can't sit and sew all day.

ANN I'm sure I'm never done finding fault from morning to night with one thing and another.

JANET Don't then.

ANN And a nice thing if I didn't! Nothing ever done in the house unless I see to it – that's what it comes to.

JANET *(spreading the cloth)* You'll drop your stitches.

ANN You never stir yourself, nor Mary neither, for that matter.

MARY I can't do much else with Tony to look after, Miss Rutherford.

JANET There's no need for her to do anything. It's not her business.

ANN Nor anybody's business, it seems to me. *(Subsiding)* I don't know what's come to Susan nowadays, she's that daft – a head like a sieve, and that clumsy-handed.

JANET Susan's got a man.

ANN Well, I never!

JANET That's what she says. It's one of the men at the Works. He hangs about on his way home from the night shift – when she ought to be doing the rooms... Susan's happy...that's why she forgot to take the milk out of the can. There's no cream for the pudding.

ANN And he's so particular about his cream.

JANET He'll have to do without for once. And what with the pie burnt – and the girdle cake like leather, if he comes in before the other's ready – I should think we'll have a fair evening.

She leaves the room.

ANN Eh, dearie – dearie. Sic doings!

MARY *(absorbed in her cap)* Never mind, Miss Rutherford.

ANN Never mind! It's well for you to talk.

MARY Janet'll see that it's all right. She always does, though she talks like that.

ANN Her and her sulky ways. There's no doing anything with her of late. She used to be bad enough as a lass, that passionate and hard to drive. She's ten times worse now she's turned quiet.

MARY Perhaps she's tired with the long walks she takes. She's been out nearly two hours this afternoon in the rain.

ANN *(turning to her knitting)* What should she have to put her out – except her own tempers.

MARY *(trying to divert her attention)* Miss Rutherford, look at Tony's cap; I've nearly finished it.

ANN *(still cross)* It's weel enough. Though what he wants wi' a lot o' bows standing up all over his head passes me.

MARY They're butterfly bows.

ANN Butterfly bows! And what'll butterfly bows do for 'n? They'll no' keep his head warm.

MARY But he looks such a darling in them. I'll put it on tomorrow when I take him out, and you'll see.

ANN London ways – that's what it is.

MARY Do north-country babies never have bows on their caps?

ANN Not in these parts. And not the Rutherfords anyway. Plain and lasting – that's the rule in this family, and we bide by it, babies and all. But you can't be expected to know, and you like a stranger in the hoose.

JANET comes in carrying a lamp and a loaf on a trencher, which she puts on the table.

MARY I've been here nearly three months.

ANN And this very night you sit wasting your time making a bit trash fit for a monkey at a fair. A body would think you would ha' learned better by now.

JANET *(quietly)* What's the matter with Mary now?

ANN We can talk, I suppose, without asking your leave?

JANET It was you that was talking. Let her be.

ANN And there you've been and put the loaf on as if it was the kitchen – and you know weel enough that gentlefolk have it set round in bits.

JANET Gentlefolk can do their own ways.

She goes out to fetch the knives.

ANN *(she gets up laboriously and goes to the table)* I'll have to do it myself as usual.

She cuts the bread and sets it round beside the plates.

MARY *(who has gone to the window and is looking out at the winter twilight)* If I'm a stranger, it's you that makes me so.

ANN Ye've no cause to speak so, lass... I'm not blamin' you. It's no' your fault that you weren't born and bred in the north country.

MARY No. I can't change that... I wonder what it's like here when the sun shines!

ANN *(who is busy with the bread)* Sun?

MARY It doesn't look as if the summer ever came here.

ANN If ye're looking for the summer in the middle o' December ye'll no' get it. Ye'll soon get used to it. Ye've happened on a bad autumn for your first, that's all.

MARY My first.

ANN Ye're a bit saft wi' livin' in the sooth, nae doubt. They tell me there's a deal of sunshine and wickedness in them parts.

MARY The people are happier, I think.

ANN Mebbees. Bein' happy'll make no porridge.

She goes back to her chair.

MARY I lived in Devonshire when I was a child, and everywhere there were lanes full of flowers – however far you went you always seemed to be at home. But here – it's all so old and stern – this great stretch of moor, and the fells – and the trees – all bent one way, crooked and huddled.

ANN *(absorbed in her knitting)* It's the sea-wind that does it.

MARY The one that's blowing now?

ANN Aye.

MARY *(with a shiver)* Shall I draw the curtains?

ANN Aye.

> **MARY** *draws the curtains. After a silence she speaks again gently.*

MARY I wonder if you'll ever get used to me enough to – like me?

ANN *(with the north-country dislike of anything demonstrative)* Like you! Sic a question – and you a kind of a relation.

MARY Myself, I mean.

ANN You're weel enough. You're a bit slip of a thing, but you're John's wife, and the mother of his bairn, and there's an end.

MARY Yes, that's all I am!

> *She takes up her work again.*

ANN Now you're talking.

MARY *(sewing)* Don't think I don't understand. John and I have been married five years. All that time Mr Rutherford never once asked to see me; if I had died, he would have been glad.

ANN I don't say that. He's a proud man, and he looked higher for his son after the eddication he'd given him. You mustn't be thinking such things.

MARY *(without bitterness)* Oh, I know all about it. If I hadn't been Tony's mother, he would never have had me inside his house. And if I hadn't been Tony's mother, I wouldn't have come. Not for anything in the world… It's wonderful how he's picked up since he got out of those stuffy lodgings.

ANN *(winding up her wool)* Well, Mr Rutherford's in the right after all.

MARY Oh yes. He's in the right.

ANN It's a bitter thing for him that's worked all his life to make a place i' the world to have his son go off and marry secret-like. Folk like him look for a return from their bairns. It's weel known that no good comes of a marriage such as yours, and it's no wonder that it takes him a bit of time to make up his mind to bide it. *(Getting up to go)* But what's done's done.

YOUNG JOHN RUTHERFORD comes in while she is speaking. He is delicate-looking and boyish in speech and manner – attractive, in spite of the fact that he is the type that has been made a gentleman of and stopped half-way in the process.

JOHN *(mimicking her tone)* So it is, Aunt Ann. Dinner's late, isn't it?

ANN He's not back yet. He's past his time. I'm sure I hope nothing's happened.

JOHN What should have happened?

ANN Who's to tell that he hasn't had an accident. Things do happen.

JOHN They do indeed. He may have jumped into a furnace.

ANN Ah, you may joke. But you never know. You never know.

She wanders out, with the vague intention of seeing to the dinner.

JOHN Cheery old soul, Aunt Ann. No one's ever five minutes late but she kills and buries them. *(Pause)* What's she been saying to you?

MARY *(sewing)* She's been talking about – us.

JOHN I should have thought that subject was about threadbare by now. *(Pause)* What's she say?

MARY The usual things. How angry your father still is, and how a marriage like ours never comes to good—

JOHN Oh, rot. Anyway, we needn't talk about it.

She looks quickly up at him and her face changes.

MARY Someone's always talking about it.

JOHN Who is?

MARY Miss Rutherford – any of them. Your father would, if he ever spoke to me at all. He looks it instead.

JOHN Oh, nonsense; you imagine things. The Guv'nor's like that with us all – it's always been so; besides, he doesn't like women – never notices them. *(Trying to make it all right)* Look here, I know it's rather beastly for you just now, but it'll be all right in time. Things are going to change, so don't you worry, little woman.

MARY What are we going to do?

JOHN Do? What should we do?

MARY Anything. To get some money of our own. To make some sort of life for ourselves, away from here.

JOHN You wait till I get this invention of mine set going. As for getting away, please remember it was you who insisted on coming. I never wanted you to.

MARY I had to come. Tony was always ailing in London.

JOHN You never left me alone till I'd crawled to the Guv'nor and asked to come back.

MARY What else was there left to do? You couldn't find work—

JOHN If you'd had patience and waited, things would have been all right.

MARY I've waited five years. I couldn't go on earning enough when Tony came.

JOHN *(sulkily)* Well, you couldn't expect me to ask the Guv'nor to keep us all three. And if I had stayed in London with you instead of coming back when he gave me the chance, what good would it have done? I'd have missed the biggest thing of my life – I know that... Anyway, I do hate this going back over it all. Beastly, sordid—

MARY *(looking before her)* I couldn't go on. I'd done it so long – long before you knew me. Day after day in an office. The crowded train morning and night – bad light – bad food – and because I did that my boy is small and delicate. I wouldn't mind but for that! There are hundreds of women doing the same thing.

But it's been nothing else all along the bare struggle for life. I sometimes think that it's the only reality in the world.

JOHN *(ill-humoured)* Whether it's the only reality or not, I call it a pretty deadly way of looking at things.

MARY It is deadly. I didn't know how deadly till I began to care for you and thought it was going to be different.

JOHN The old story.

MARY No, no, we won't look back. But oh, John, I do so dreadfully want things for Tony. *(**JOHN** begins to move about the room)* I didn't mind when there was only ourselves. But when he was coming I began to think, to look at the other children – children of people in our position in London – taught to work before they'd had time to learn what work means – with the manhood ground out of them before ever it came. And I thought how that was what we had to give our child, you and I... When your father forgave you for marrying me, and said you might come here, it seemed like a chance. And there's nothing, nothing – except this place you call home.

JOHN Hang it all—

MARY Oh, I know it's big – there's food and warmth, but it's like a prison! There's not a scrap of love in the whole house. Your father! – no one's any right to be what he is – never questioned, never answered back – like God! And the rest of you just living round him – neither children, nor men and women – hating each other.

JOHN *(turning to look at her with a sort of wonder)* Don't exaggerate. Whatever has set you off talking like this?

MARY Because I'm always thinking about it.

JOHN You've never had a home of your own, and you don't make excuses for family life – everybody knows it's like that more or less.

MARY And you've lived with it always – you can't see it as I do.

JOHN I do see it. And it's jolly unpleasant – I'm not arguing about that—

MARY Don't you see that life in this house is intolerable?

JOHN Well, frankly, no, I don't. That is, I don't see why you should find it so. After what you've been used to... It's all very well to abuse my people, and I sympathise with you in a way – no one dislikes them more than I do. I know Janet's got a filthy temper, and Aunt Ann – well, she hasn't moved on with the rest of us, poor old soul, that's the long and the short of it. As for the Guv'nor – it's no use beginning to apologise for him.

MARY Apologise!

JOHN Well, that's about what you seem to expect. I've told you I quite see that it isn't over pleasant for you, and you might leave it at that, I think. You do drive at one so...and you seem to forget how ill I've been.

MARY I don't forget. But don't you see we may go on like this for twenty years doing nothing?

JOHN Do you suppose I wouldn't have done something? Do you suppose I didn't mean to do something, if I hadn't been knocked over just at the critical moment? *(injured)* Do you suppose I wouldn't rather have been working than lying on my back all these weeks?

MARY *(quietly)* How about all the other weeks?

JOHN Good heavens, what more could I do than I have done? Here have I hit on a thing worth thousands – a thing that any glass-maker would give his ears to have the working of. And you talk to me about making money – and a life of our own. Good Lord! We're going to be rich – rich, once it's set going.

MARY *(unimpressed)* Have you told Mr Rutherford about it?

JOHN Yes. At least, I've told him what it is – I haven't told him how it's done – naturally... He won't listen to me – it's like talking to a lump of granite. He'll find he'll have to listen before long... I've set Martin on to him.

MARY Why Martin?

JOHN Because he helped me to work it out. And because he happens to be the one person in the world the Guv'nor ever listens to.

MARY *(looking up)* He trusts Martin, doesn't he? Absolutely.

JOHN Oh, Lord! Yes. Martin can do no wrong. The Guv'nor'll listen to him all right.

MARY *(resuming her work)* When is he going to tell him?

JOHN Oh, directly he gets a chance. He may have done it already.

MARY *(putting down her sewing)* Today? Then Martin really believes there's something in it?

JOHN *(indignantly)* Something in it! My dear Mary, I know you don't mean to be, but you are most fearfully irritating. Here have I told you over and over again that I'm going to make my fortune, and because someone else agrees with me you're kind enough to believe what I say. One would think you had no faith in me.

MARY *(giving it up as hopeless)* I'm sorry. We won't talk of it any more. I've said it all so often – said it till you're sick of hearing it, and it's no good.

JOHN Molly, don't be cross... I don't mean to be a brute, but it is a bit disappointing, isn't it? When I really have found the right thing at last, to find you so lukewarm about it. Because it really is this time. It'll change everything; and you shall do what you like and enjoy yourself as much as you want to – and forget all about those filthy years in Walton Street. *(He comes to her and puts his arm round her)* There, don't be a little fool. What are you making?

MARY A cap for Tony.

JOHN Dear little beggar, isn't he?

MARY Yes... Don't say things to please me, John.

JOHN I'm not. I do think he's a dear little beggar. *(Pleased with himself)* We'll be as happy as kings by and by.

MARY As happy as we were at first?

JOHN Happier – we'll have money.

MARY We couldn't be happier. *(She sits with her hands in her lap, her mouth wistful)* What a pair of babies we were, weren't we?

JOHN Oh, I don't know.

MARY What – blunderers! I thought it was so different – and I dare say you did, too, though you never said so. I suppose it's really true what they think here – that we'd no business to marry and have a child when we'd nothing to give him when he came.

JOHN What a little worrit you are.

MARY I do worry, John – you don't know how much.

JOHN But what about?

MARY Tony.

JOHN You funny little thing. Surely there's time enough to think about Tony; he's just four months old.

MARY Yes, but to me – I suppose every woman thinks about her baby like that – till he's a boy and a man and a child all in one – only he never grows old. *(In a practical tone)* How long will it take?

JOHN How long will what take?

MARY Your invention. *(Looks up quickly)* I mean – don't be cross – will it be months – or years before it pays?

JOHN *(moving away)* I really can't say – it depends. If the Guv'nor has the sense to see things my way – it depends.

He takes a cigarette.

MARY I see. You will work at it, won't you? Make it go?

JOHN *(striking a light)* There's no work to be done. All I've got to do is to sit down and let someone pay for it.

MARY Sit down? It seems so much to us, doesn't it? Everything—

JOHN *(who has burnt his finger)* It means my getting the whip-hand of the Guv'nor for once in my life. *(Irritably)* And it means my getting away from your incessant nagging at me about the kid – and money.

MARY John!

JOHN *(sharply)* After all, it isn't very pleasant for me having you dependent on the Guv'nor and being reminded of it every other day. I don't choose this kind of life, I can tell you. If you're sick of it, God knows I am.

While he is speaking, **ANN** *drifts into the room again.*

ANN There you are – smoking again; and you know what the doctor said. Mary, tell him he's not to.

MARY John must do as he likes.

JOHN I must have something; my nerves are all on edge.

ANN Weel, ye can't expect to be right all of a sudden. When I think o' the Sunday night ye was so bad, I never thought to see ye standin' there now.

JOHN *(injured)* I shouldn't worry about that. I don't suppose anyone would have been much the worse if I had pegged out.

ANN Whatever makes you say a thing like that?

JOHN Mary. Yes, you do, Mary. To hear you talk one would think I was no good. How do you suppose I've made an invention if I were the rotter you think me?

MARY I didn't say that – I didn't say that.

ANN An invention's weel enough if you're not mistaken.

JOHN Mistaken!

ANN Ah, but older people nor you make mistakes. There was old Green – I mind him fiddlin' on wi' a lot of old cogs and screws half his time, trying to find oot the way to prevent a railway train going off the line. And when he did find it and took it to show it to someone as knawed aboot such things, it was so sartin sure not to go off the line that the wheels wouldn't turn roond at all. A poor, half-baked body he was, and his wife without a decent black to show herself in o' Sundays.

JOHN I'll undertake that my wheels will go round.

ANN If it's such a wonderful thing, why hasn't someone thought of it afore? Answer me that.

JOHN You might say that of any new idea that ever came into the world.

ANN Of course, if you set up to know more about glass-making than your father that's been at it ever since he was a bairn...

JOHN It isn't a case of knowing. I've a much better chance because I don't know. It's the duffers who get hold of the best things – stumble over them in the dark, as I did. It makes my blood run cold to think how easily I could have missed it, of all the people who must have looked straight at it time after time, and never seen it. *(Contemptuously)* Hullo, Dick!

RICHARD RUTHERFORD *has come in from the hall. He wears the regulation clergyman's clothes and looks older than* **JOHN**, *though he is in reality the younger by a couple of years. He is habitually overworked, and his face has the rather pathetic look of an overweighted youth that finds life too much for its strength. His manner is extremely simple and sincere, which enables him to use priggish phrases without offence. He comes to the table while* **JOHN** *is speaking, looks from him to* **ANN**, *then at the butter, sugar, and bread in turn.*

DICK *(very tired)* Dinner?

JOHN *(mimicking him)* Not imminent.

DICK Will it be long?

ANN *(crossly)* Ye'll just have to bide quiet till it comes.

DICK *(gently)* Ah! ...In that case I think I'll just—

He takes a piece of bread and moves towards the door.

ANN You look fair done...

DICK I've had a tiring day. *(To* **MARY***)* Where is Janet?

MARY In the kitchen. *(She looks at him intently)* Why did you ask? Do you want her?

DICK *(uncertainly)* No, no. I thought she might have gone out. It's best for her not to go out after dark.

ANN You can't sit in your room i' this cold.

DICK I'll put on a coat. It's quiet there.

JOHN You'll have time to write your sermon before he comes in, I dare say.

DICK *(simply)* Oh, I've done that, such as it is.

He leaves the room, eating his bread as he goes.

JOHN *(irritably)* This is a damned uncomfortable house. I'm starving.

ANN It's Committee day.

JOHN He'll be having the whole Board on his toes as usual, I suppose.

ANN That Board'll be the death of him. When I think of the old days when he'd no one to please but himself!

JOHN He's stood it for five years. I wouldn't – being badgered by a lot of directors who know as much about glass-making as you do.

ANN That's all very well. But when you borrow money you've got to be respectful one way and another. If he hadn't gone to the Bank how would Rutherford's ha' gone on?

JOHN *(who has taken up the newspaper and is half reading it as he talks)* Why should it go on?

ANN *(sharply)* What's that?

JOHN Why didn't he sell the place when he could have made a decent profit?

ANN *(scandalised)* Sell Rutherford's? Just you let your father hear you.

JOHN I don't care if he does. I never can imagine why he hangs on – working his soul out year after year.

ANN *(conclusively)* It's his duty!

She resumes her knitting.

JOHN Duty – rot! He likes it. He's gone on too long. He couldn't stop and rest if he tried. When I make a few thousands out of this little idea of mine I'm going to have everything I want, and forget all about the dirt and the ugliness, the clatter and bang of the machinery, the sickening hot smell of the furnaces – all the things I've hated from my soul.

ANN *(who has become absorbed in a dropped stich)* Aye weel… there's another strike at Rayner's, they tell me.

JOHN Yes. Eight hundred men. That's the second this year.

ANN You don't think it'll happen here, do you?

JOHN I can't say. They're smashing things at Rayner's.

ANN It'll no' come here. The men think too much of your father for that.

JOHN I'm not so sure.

ANN There was the beginnings of a strike once, years ago, and he stopped it then. The men at the furnaces struck work – said it was too hard for 'n. And your father he went doon into the caves and took his coat off afore them all, and pitched joost half as much coal again as the best of 'em – now!

JOHN Yes, that's the sort of argument they can see – it catches hold of the brute in them. If the Guv'nor had sat quietly in his office and sent his ultimatum through the usual channels, he would have been the owner of Rutherford's, and the strike would have run its course. Shovelling coal in his shirt with his muscles straining, and the sweat pouring off him, he was 'wor John' – and there's three cheers for his fourteen stone of beef and muscle. That was all very well – thirty years ago.

ANN And what's to hinder it now?

JOHN Oh, the Guv'nor was a bit of a hero then – an athlete, a runner. The men who worked for him all the week crowded to see him run on Saturday afternoons, Martin's told me. But when all's said and done, Rutherford's is a money-making machine. And the Guv'nor's the only man who doesn't know it. He's getting old.

ANN *(crossly)* To hear you talk, a body would think we were all going to die tomorrow. Your father's a year younger nor me – now! And a fine up-standing man forbye.

JOHN *(who is looking at himself in the glass above the mantelpiece)* Oh, he knows how to manage a pack of savages.

ANN There's not one of 'em today or thirty years ago but'll listen to him.

JOHN He'd knock anyone down who didn't.

> JANET *comes in with a tray and begins to set cups and saucers on the table.*

ANN They all stood by him when the trouble came, every one of 'em. And he's climbed up steady ever since, and never looked ahint him. And now you've got your invention it'll no be long now – if it's all you think it. Ah, it 'ud be grand to see Rutherford's like old times again.

JOHN Rutherford's... *(he speaks half seriously, half to tease* **ANN***)* Aunt Ann, have you ever in your life – just for a moment at the back of your mind – wished Rutherford's at the bottom of the Tyne?

ANN gazes at him in silence. When she speaks again it is as to a foolish child.

ANN Are you taking your medicine reg'lar?

JOHN Yes. But have you ever heard of Moloch? No. Well, Moloch was a sort of a god – some time ago, you know, before Dick and his kind came along. They built his image with an ugly head ten times the size of a real head, with great wheels instead of legs, and set him up in the middle of a great dirty town. *(*JANET*, busy at the table, stops to listen, raising her eyes almost for the first time)* And they thought him a very important person indeed, and made sacrifices to him – human sacrifices – to keep him going, you know. Out of every family they set aside one child to be an offering to him when it was big enough, and at last it became a sort of honour to be dedicated in this way, so much so, that the victims gave themselves gladly to be crushed out of life under the great wheels. That was Moloch.

There is a silence. **JANET** *speaks eagerly.*

JANET Where did you get that?

JOHN Get what?

JANET What you've been saying.

JOHN Everybody knows it.

JANET Dedicated – we're dedicated – all of us – to Rutherford's. And being respected in Grantley.

ANN Talk, talk – chatter, chatter. Words never mended nothing that I knows on.

JOHN *(who is tired of the subject)* Talk – if I hadn't you to talk to, Aunt Ann, or Mary, I think I'd talk to the door-post.

JANET *(who has slipped back into her dull listlessness)* And just as much good would come of it, I dare say.

ANN And who are you to say it? You got no book-learning like him – and no invention neither.

JANET *(who is laying forks round the table)* How do you know he's got an invention?

ANN Because he says so, o' course – how else? It's a secret.

JANET John always had a secret. He used to sell them to me when we were little. And when I'd given him whatever it was he'd taken a fancy to, there was no secret. Nothing worth paying for, anyway.

JOHN Oh, shut up.

ANN *(as if they were children)* Now, now. Don't quarrel.

JANET We're not quarrelling.

JOHN Yes, we are. And you began it.

JANET I didn't. I only said what anyone can see. *(Scornfully)* You make an invention. Likely.

JOHN A lot you know about it.

JANET If you did, you'd muck it somehow, just as you do everything.

ANN *(querulously)* Bairns! Bairns! One would think you'd never growed up.

JOHN *(angrily to JANET)* I wish you'd keep quiet if you can't say anything decent. You never open your mouth except to say something disagreeable. First there's Mary throwing cold water, then you come in.

JANET I'm not any more disagreeable than anyone else. We're all disagreeable if it comes to that. All except Susan.

ANN Susan's not one of the family! A common servant lass.

JANET Like me.

ANN *(using the family threat)* Just you let your father hear you.

JANET We do the same things.

ANN Susan's paid for it. Whoever gave you a farthing?

JANET *(bitterly)* Aye!

ANN Has she made another girdle cake?

JANET I didn't notice. She's probably talking to her young man at the gate.

JOHN Susan with a young man!

ANN Yes, indeed – a nice thing, and her turned forty.

JOHN Ugliest woman I ever saw bar none. Who is it? Not Martin surely! *(*JANET *stops suddenly and looks at him)* I've noticed he's been making excuses to come about lately, and he's taken the cottage at the Tarn.

JANET *(with a sudden stillness)* It isn't Martin.

JOHN Well, if it is, the Guv'nor would soon put a stop to it.

JANET Put a stop to what?

JOHN Martin getting married – if it's that he's after.

JANET What right's he to interfere?

JOHN Right – nonsense. Martin practically lives at the Works as it is. If he had a wife he'd get to be just like the other men – hankering after going home at the proper time, and all that.

ANN *(preparing to leave the room)* You and your gossip – and the dinner spoiling every minute. *(With a parting shot at* JANET*)* It's a good thing nobody's married you – a nice hoose you'd make without me to look to everything.

She fusses out.

JOHN Married! Cheer up, Janet! Thirty-five last birthday, isn't it?

MARY John!

JANET *(her voice hard)* No, it isn't. It's thirty-six.

JOHN You'll make a happy home for someone yet. No one's asked you so far, I suppose?

JANET Who's there been to ask me?

JOHN Oh, I don't know. I suppose you have been kept pretty close. Other girls manage it, don't they?

JANET I don't know other girls.

JOHN Mary caught me.

JANET I don't know anybody – you know that. No one in. Grantley's good enough for us, and we're not good enough for the other kind.

JOHN Speak for yourself.

JANET Oh, we're all alike; don't you fret. Why hasn't young Squire Earnshaw invited you to shoot with him again? He did once – when none of his grand friends were there.

JOHN *pretends not to hear.*

I know why.

JOHN Oh, you know a lot, don't you?

JANET It was because you pretended – pretended you knew the folk he talked about, because you'd shown them over the Works once when father was away. Pretended you said 'parss' for pass every day. I heard you. And I saw the difference. Gentlemen are natural. Being in company doesn't put them about. They don't say 'thank you' to servants neither, not like you do to Susan.

JOHN Oh, shut up, will you?

JANET I wouldn't pretend, whatever I did – mincing round like a monkey.

ANN *(coming in from the kitchen)* Now, now. That's the door, isn't it?

They all listen. A voice is heard outside, then the outer door opens.

JOHN Father.

JANET Martin.

There is the sound of a stick being put into the umbrella stand; then **JOHN RUTHERFORD** *comes in, followed by* **MARTIN**. *He is a heavily-built man of sixty, with a heavy lined face and tremendous shoulders – a typical north countryman. There is a distinct change in the manner of the whole family as he comes in and walks straight to his desk as if the door had scarcely interrupted his walk.* **MARTIN** *is a good-looking man of the best type of working* man. *Very simple in manner and hearing – about forty years of age. He touches his forelock to the family and stands beside the door with nothing servile in either action.*

RUTHERFORD *(talking as he comes in)* ...and it's got to be managed somehow. Lads are wanted and lads'll have to be found. Only six out of the seventeen furnaces started the first shift o' Monday.

MARTIN Grey couldn't start at all last week for want o' lads.

RUTHERFORD What's got them? Ten years ago you could have had fifty for the asking, and taken your pick. And now here's the work waiting to be done, and half the hands we want to do it lounging about Grantley with their hands in their breeches pockets, the beggars. What do they think they're bred for?

MARTIN There's too many of 'em making for the towns, that's it. It's lighter work.

RUTHERFORD Measuring out bits of tape for the lasses, in a boiled shirt and the like. Just remind me to give the men a word o' wages time o' Saturday. They got to keep their lads at home as long as they're wanted at Rutherford's. *(Turning papers and a bunch of keys out of his pocket on to the desk)* The new lear man's shaping all right then.

MARTIN Dale? Knows as much aboot a pot-arch as I knows aboot a flying-machine.

RUTHERFORD Why didn't you tell me before?

MARTIN I thought I'd wait to give him a trial. I took a look at the flues myself to make sure it wasn't them at fault. He can't get the heat up properly, and the pots are put into the furnaces afore they're furnace heat. They'll all be broke one o' these days.

RUTHERFORD We'd better take on Ford.

MARTIN He finishes at Cardiff Saturday.

RUTHERFORD He'll do, I suppose?

MARTIN *(feeling in his pocket and pulling out a leather purse or bag)* You couldn't get a better man for the job in all Tyneside. There's the ten pound young Henderson had out o' the till.

He counts it out on the desk.

RUTHERFORD What! He's given it up?

MARTIN Aye. Leastways, I took it off him.

RUTHERFORD Has he owned to it?

MARTIN Sure enough. Said he hadn't gone for to do it. Cried like a bairn, he did.

JOHN *(from his arm-chair by the fire)* Henderson? Has he been stealing?

MARTIN Aye, Mr John. I caught him at it i' the office – at dinner-time when there's nobody much aboot – wi' his hands i' the till.

JOHN Dirty little sweep! Have you kicked him out?

RUTHERFORD *(pausing with his hand on his cash box)* I suppose there's no doubt he's a bad 'un?

MARTIN Bred and born.

RUTHERFORD No use giving him another chance.

MARTIN Throwed away on the likes o' him.

RUTHERFORD *(locking the box and putting it in a drawer)* Ah... Well, if he comes back, turn him away. Everything ready for the pot-setting in the morning?

MARTIN Aye, sir. The night shift'll set four when they stop, and the other shift'll set the others a bit later.

RUTHERFORD You'll be there to see them do it?

MARTIN Surely.

RUTHERFORD *(with a curious softening in his voice)* When'll you get your rest?

MARTIN Plenty o' time for that, sir.

RUTHERFORD *(crossing to the fire)* We'll have you on strike one o' these days, Martin.

MARTIN *(turning to go)* Not me, sir. When you begin to spare yourself you can begin to think about sparing me. And next week things'll go easier... Is that all for the night, sir?

RUTHERFORD *(wearily)* Aye. Goodnight to ye. *(He has taken his pipe from the rack above the mantelpiece and is filling it)* You've further to go now ye're in the Tarn Cottage.

There is a slight pause before MARTIN *replies.*

MARTIN Aye. A bit, mebbee.

RUTHERFORD *(lighting his pipe)* I – should ha' – thought you'd had done better to stick to your old one – near at hand; but you know your own business best.

MARTIN It's weel enough.

ANN Now Martin's here, can he no take a look at the range? Susan canna get the oven to go.

JANET *(to* ANN*)* The oven's all right.

RUTHERFORD *(with a complete change of voice and manner)* Now what's that got to do with Martin?

ANN *(subsiding)* He could tell Baines to send up a man i' the mornin'.

RUTHERFORD That's not Martin's business – you must send word to Baines himself.

MARTIN I could easy take a look at it while I'm here, sir. It 'ud save you sending.

RUTHERFORD *(wearily)* Oh, all right. If you want a job.

ANN Janet, go and show Martin.

MARTIN *turns at the door and looks for her to pass out before him.*

JANET *(standing motionless)* Susan can show him.

MARTIN *goes, closing the door.*

RUTHERFORD Any letters?

ANN *(flurried)* Yes. They're somewheres. Janet—

RUTHERFORD *(with the sudden irritation of a tired man)* Bless me, can't I have a simple thing like that done for me? How often have I said to put them in one place and stick to it?

(**JANET** *discovers the letters on the small table by the door and brings them to him. He sits on the settle and stretches out his legs*) Here, take them off for me. I'm dead beat.

After a moment's silent revolt she kneels and begins to unlace his boots.

He looks at her bent sullen face.

Ah! Sulky, are ye?

She makes no answer.

'Ud like to tell me to take them off myself, I dare say. And I been working the day long for you. (*Getting irritated at her touch*) Spoilt – that's what you are, my lass. (*Opening a letter*) What's this? A polite letter from the vicar, eh? Damn polite – a new organ – that's his trouble – thinks I'd like to help pay for it. (*He throws it across the hearthrug to* **JOHN**) There's a job for you – you're idle enough. Write and tell His Reverence to go to the devil and ask him for an organ. Or mebbee Richard'll like to do it, as he's his curate. (*To* **JANET**) Let be, let be.

He takes his boots off painfully one with the other.

ANN (*plaintively*) I'm sure the vicar came in pleasant enough not a week gone, and asked for 'ee—

RUTHERFORD Asked for my money, you mean. They're civil enough when they want anything, the lot of them. (*To* **JANET** *– sarcastically, as she carries the boots away*) Thank 'ee kindly.

He gets up and puts his slippers on. **ANN** *speaks in a flurried whisper to* **JOHN**.

ANN John, you've got your father's chair.

JOHN (*gets up*) Sorry.

RUTHERFORD (*drags the chair up to the table, and sits down as if he were tired out. He looks at* **JOHN** *with a curiously interested expression as he lounges across*) Feeling better?

JOHN (*uneasy and consequently rather swaggering*) Oh, I'm still a bit shaky about the knees.

RUTHERFORD You'll be coming back to work, I suppose. There's plenty to be done. How's the little lad?

JOHN I don't know – all right, I suppose. Isn't he, Mary?

MARY Mr Rutherford asked you.

JOHN But I don't know...

RUTHERFORD *looks at* MARY, *she at him; there is a pause.*

RUTHERFORD *(busy with his letters)* I thought Gibson had forbidden you to smoke?

JOHN *rebels for a moment, then throws his cigarette into the fire, with an action like a petted child.*

JOHN I must do something.

RUTHERFORD What have you been busy with today? ...This – metal o' yours? Eh?

JOHN *(evasively)* Aunt Ann's been talking about it.

ANN *(meaning well)* We've joost been saying how it'll all come right now – all the bother. John'll do it – Rutherford's'll be itself again.

RUTHERFORD Martin tells me you've hit on a good thing – a big thing... I've got to hear more about it, eh?

JOHN If you like.

RUTHERFORD What's that?

He looks up slowly under his eyebrows – a long curious look, as if he saw the first possibility of opposition.

JOHN *(going over to the fireplace)* Can't we have dinner?

ANN You're getting back your appetite. That's a good sign.

RUTHERFORD Dinner can wait. *(He sweeps a space clear on the table and puts his letters down.* JANET *presently sits down resigned to a family row.* MARY *listens throughout intently, her eyes constantly fixed on* JOHN*)* I'm a business man, and I like to know how I stand. *(Launching at* JOHN*)* Now – what d'ye mean?

JOHN I don't understand you, sir.

RUTHERFORD What's there to understand?

JOHN *(his manner gradually slipping into that of a child afraid of its father)* Well, I've been away from the Works for two months. Before we begin to talk about the other thing, I'd like to know what's doing.

RUTHERFORD What's that got to do with it? You never have known what's doing.

JOHN I think I ought to be told – now.

RUTHERFORD Now! That's it, is it? You want a bone flung to your dignity! Well, here it is. Things are bad.

JOHN Really bad?

RUTHERFORD For the present. These colliery strikes one on top of another, for one thing. Rayner's drew the ponies out of the pit this afternoon.

JOHN It'll about smash them, won't it?

RUTHERFORD Mebbee. The question is how it affects us.

JOHN Oh! We get coal from them?

RUTHERFORD I should have thought you'd ha' picked up that much – in five years.

JOHN Stoking isn't my business.

RUTHERFORD You might have noticed the name on the trucks – you see it every day of your life. Well, yes – we get our coal from them... What then?

JOHN Well – what's going to happen? How bad is it?

RUTHERFORD I said – bad for the present. The balance-sheet for the year's just been drawn up and shows a loss of four thousand on last year's working. It's not a big loss, considering what's been against us – those Americans dumping all that stuff in the spring – we had to stop that little game, and it cost us something to do it. Then the price of materials has gone up, there's a difference there. *(Irritably, answering his own thoughts)* It's not ruin, bless us – it's simply a question of work and sticking together; but the Bank's rather more difficult to manage than usual. There's not one of 'em would sacrifice a shilling of their own to keep the old place going – they want their fees reg'lar. That's their idea of the commercial enterprise they're always talking about. It's the pulse they keep their finger on – when it misses a beat, they come crowding round with their hands up like a lot of damned old women... Well, well! Something's wanted to pull things together... Now – this idea of yours. Martin tells me it's worth something.

JOHN *(nettled)* Worth something? It's worth thousands a year to anyone who works it properly.

RUTHERFORD *(with his half smile)* Thousands! That's a fair margin. *(Drily)* What's your calculation in figures?

JOHN That depends on the scale it's worked on.

RUTHERFORD *(as to a child)* Yes – so I supposed. What's your preliminary cost?

JOHN *(getting nervous)* Nothing – as far as I know. I can't say for certain – something like that.

RUTHERFORD Something like nothing; and on something like nothing you're going to show a profit of thousands a year on a single metal. *(Drily)* Sounds like a beautiful dream, doesn't it? About your cost of working now – that should run you into something?

JOHN *(who is getting annoyed)* Thirty per cent less than what you're working at now.

RUTHERFORD Indeed... May I ask where and how you've carried out your experiments?

JOHN *(uneasily)* I didn't mention it to you. A year ago I got a muffle furnace. I've worked with it from time to time, in the old pot-loft.

RUTHERFORD Paid for it by any chance?

JOHN Not yet.

RUTHERFORD How did you manage for coals now?

JOHN I – took what I wanted from the heap.

RUTHERFORD Ah, and your materials – I suppose you took what you wanted of those too? Well, I've no objection, if you can make it good. *(Suddenly)* What's your recipe?

JOHN I haven't – I'm not prepared to say.

There is a silence. **ANN** *lowers her knitting with an alarmed look.*

RUTHERFORD *(heavily)* A week or two ago in this room you told me it was perfected – ready for working tomorrow.

JOHN Yes – I told you so.

RUTHERFORD *(suppressed)* What d'ye mean? ...Come, come, sir – I'm your father, I want an answer to my question – a plain answer, if you can give one.

JOHN *(in a high-pitched, nervous voice)* I – I'm a business man, and I want to know where I stand.

RUTHERFORD *breaks into a laugh.*

Oh, you turn me into an impudent schoolboy, but I'm not. I'm a man, with a thing in my mind worth a fortune.

ANN John! *(asserting her authority)* You must tell your father.

JOHN *(very excited)* I shan't tell him till I've taken out my patent, so there!

There is a pause – **RUTHERFORD** *stares at his son.*

RUTHERFORD *(heavily)* What d'ye mean?

JOHN I mean what I say. I want my price.

RUTHERFORD Your price – your price? *(bringing his fist down on the table)* Damn your impudence, sir. A whippersnapper like you to talk about your price.

JOHN *(losing his temper)* I'm not a whippersnapper. I've got something to sell and you want to buy it, and there's an end.

RUTHERFORD To buy? To sell? And this to your father?

JOHN To any man who wants what I've made.

There is a dead silence on this, broken only by an involuntary nervous movement from the rest of the family. Then **RUTHERFORD** *speaks without moving.*

RUTHERFORD Ah! So that's your line, is it? ...This is what I get for all I've done for you... This is the result of the schooling I give you.

JOHN *(with an attempt at a swagger)* I suppose you mean Harrow.

RUTHERFORD It was two hundred pound – that's what I mean.

JOHN And you gave me a year of it!

RUTHERFORD And a lot of good you've got of it... What ha' you done with it? Idled your time away wi' your books o' poetry when you should ha' been working. Married a wife who bears you a bairn you can't keep. *(At a movement from* **MARY***)* Aye – hard words mebbee. What will you do for your son when the time comes? I've toiled and sweated to give you a name you'd be proud to own – worked early and late, toiled like a dog when other men were taking their ease – plotted and planned to get my chance, taken it and held it when it come till I could ha' burst with the struggle. Sell! You talk o' selling to me, when everything you'll ever make couldn't pay back the life I've given to you!

JOHN Oh, I know, I know.

ANN You mustn't answer your father, John.

JOHN Well, after all, I didn't ask to be born.

RUTHERFORD Nor did the little lad, God help him.

JOHN *(rapidly)* Look here, Father – why did you send me to Harrow?

RUTHERFORD Why? To make a gentleman of you, and because I thought they'd teach you better than the Grammar School. I was mistaken.

JOHN They don't turn out good clerks and office boys.

RUTHERFORD What's that?

JOHN I've been both for five years. Only I've had no salary.

RUTHERFORD You've been put to learn your business like any other young fellow. I began at the bottom – you've got to do the same. There'll not be two masters at Rutherford's while I'm on my legs.

JOHN That's it, that's it. You make a servant of me.

RUTHERFORD What do you suppose your work's worth to Rutherford's? Tell me that.

JOHN What's that matter now? I've done with it. I've found a way out.

RUTHERFORD A way out – of what?

JOHN *(rather taken aback)* Well – you don't suppose I'd choose to live here all my life?

ANN *(taking it personally)* And why not, pray?

RUTHERFORD Your father has lived here, and your grandfather before you. It's your inheritance – can't you realise that? – what you've got to come to when I'm underground. We've made it for you, stone by stone, penny by penny, fighting through thick and thin for close on a hundred years.

JOHN Well, after all, I can't help what you and grandfather chose to do.

RUTHERFORD Chose to do! There's no chose to do. The thing's there. You're my son – my son that's got to come after me.

JOHN Oh, it's useless. Our ideas of life are utterly different.

RUTHERFORD Ideas of life! What do you know about life?

JOHN Oh, nothing, of course.

RUTHERFORD If you did, you'd soon stop having ideas about it. Life! I've had nigh on sixty years of it, and I'll tell you. Life's work – keeping your head up and your heels down. Sleep, and begetting children, rearing them up to work when you're gone – that's life. And when you know better than the God who made you, you can begin to ask what you're going to get by it. And you'll get more work and six foot of earth at the end of it.

JOHN And that's what you mean me to do, is it?

RUTHERFORD It's what you've got to do – or starve. You're my son – you've got to come after me.

JOHN Look here, Father. You tell me all this. Just try and see things my way for once. Take the Works. I know you've done it all, built it up, and all that – and you're quite right to be proud of it. But I – I don't like the place, that's the long and the short of it. It's not worth my while. After all, I've got myself to think of – my own life. If I'd done that sooner, by Jove! I'd have been a jolly sight better off. I'd not have married, for one thing. *(With a glance at* **MARY***)* Not that I regret that. You talk about what you did when you were young. You've told me the sort of time you've had – nothing but grind, grind, since the time you could do anything. And what have you got by it? What have you got? I have myself to think of. I want a run for my money – your money, I suppose it is – other fellows do. And I've made this thing myself, off my own bat – and – and *(ending lamely)* – I don't see why I shouldn't have a look in... On my own account...

There is an uncomfortable silence.

RUTHERFORD *(in a new tone)* You're going to take out a patent, you say?

JOHN *(taking this as friendly)* Yes.

RUTHERFORD Know anything about Patent Law?

JOHN Well, no – not yet.

RUTHERFORD It's very simple, and wonderfully cheap – three pound for three years. At the end of three years, you can always extend the time if you want to – no difficulty about that.

JOHN Oh, no.

RUTHERFORD But you can't patent a metal.

JOHN I don't see why not.

RUTHERFORD What's the use if you do?

JOHN It's the same as anything else. I take out a patent for a certain receipt, and I can come down on anyone who uses it.

RUTHERFORD And prove that they've used it?

JOHN They have to find out what it is first. It's not likely I'm going to give the show away. *(Pause)*

RUTHERFORD But you want to sell, you say.

JOHN Yes.

RUTHERFORD How are you going to do that without giving it away? ...Suppose you go to one of the big chaps – Miles of Cardiff, for example. 'Here you are,' you say. 'I've got an idea worth a fortune. Give me a fortune and I'll tell you what it is.' He's not going to buy a pig in a poke any more than I am. People have a way of thinking they're going to make their fortunes, d'ye see? But those people aren't generally the sort you let loose in your glasshouse.

JOHN Of course, I shall make inquiries about all that. I can't say till I know.

RUTHERFORD Do you remember a little thing of mine – an invention you would call it. Did ye ever happen to see it?

JOHN Yes. Martin showed it to me once.

RUTHERFORD What's your opinion of that now – as a business man?

JOHN Of course, it had the makings of a good thing – anyone could see that.

RUTHERFORD Nobody did. I was nineteen at the time – a lad. Like you, I hadn't the money to run it myself. Clinton, the American people, got hold of it, and sold seven hundred thousand the first six months in New York alone. *(He gets up and addresses the room, generally)* Dinner in ten minutes.

JOHN Surely you could have got someone to take it up – an obvious thing like that?

RUTHERFORD *(drily)* That's how it worked out in my case. *(He moves slowly to the door)*

JOHN You don't believe I can do what I say.

RUTHERFORD I can't tell – nor can you.

JOHN *(high-handed)* Oh, very well then. What are we talking about?

RUTHERFORD You undertake to produce ordinary white metal at a third of the usual cost – that's it, isn't it? You've worked this out in a muffle furnace. My experience of muffle furnaces is that they're excellent for experimenting in a very small way. A child can hit on an idea for a metal – provided he's materials at his command, and knows a bit about chemistry. But no man living can estimate the cost of that idea until it's worked out on a big scale. Your recipe, as it stands, isn't worth the paper it's written on.

As **RUTHERFORD** *moves again towards the door* **JOHN** *makes a movement to stop him.*

JOHN Father, look here. Here's an offer.

RUTHERFORD Thank you kindly.

JOHN If you'll let me have a pot in one of the big furnaces for a trial – I swear to you, on my honour, I'll let you see the result without touching it, after I've put in the materials. You can clay the pots up – seal them, if you like. Let me do it tomorrow; I can't stand hanging on like this.

RUTHERFORD Tomorrow! Impossible.

JOHN Why not?

RUTHERFORD You can't come down to the Works in this weather. You'd catch cold, and be laid up again.

JOHN The day after then – next week – or, why not? – let Martin do it.

RUTHERFORD Martin? *(he turns to look at* **JOHN**, *struck by a new thought)*

JOHN Why not? He can do it as well as I can.

RUTHERFORD Martin? ...He knows then?

JOHN *(surprised)* Why, he talked to you about it, didn't he?

RUTHERFORD Yes, yes. But – he's got the recipe?

JOHN Yes – there's no difficulty at all. Let him mix the metal and clay her up, and you can open her yourself. Then you'll see. You'll take Martin's word for it, I suppose? Only, for Heaven's sake, give me a fair chance.

RUTHERFORD *(moving suddenly)* Fair chance be damned, sir. You've said your say, and I've said mine. Think it over!

He goes out, leaving **JOHN** *standing staring after him.*

JOHN *(under his breath as the door closes)* Oh, go to the devil!

ANN For shame to speak so. Just let him hear you. And there, dinner'll be as dry as a bone, and I've waited so long I don't feel as if I could touch a morsel. You might keep your business till we'd had something to eat, I think. *(She hurries out)*

JANET *(with a sort of admiration)* Now you've done it.

JOHN Done it! I've jolly well let him know what I think – and high time, too. *(Brokenly)* It isn't fair – it isn't fair. Old bully. What am I going to do?

JANET *(dropping into her usual tone)* What you've always done, I suppose.

JOHN What's that?

JANET Say you're sorry. It's the soonest way back.

JOHN I'm not going back. Sooner than give in, I'll starve. I don't care. I'll go to London, Canada, anywhere. He shan't have me, to grind the life out of me by inches and he shan't have my metal. If he thinks he's going to pick my brains and give me nothing for it; he'll find himself jolly well mistaken. I don't care. Once and for all, I'm going to make a stand. And he can jolly well go to the devil.

MARY *speaks for the first time, in a low voice.*

MARY What are you making a stand for?

JOHN *(stopping to look at her)* Good Lord, Mary, haven't you been listening?

MARY Yes, I've been listening. You said you wanted your price. What is your price?

JANET All the profits and none of the work – that's John's style. *(She sits on settle, her chin on her hands)*

JOHN A lot you know about it.

MARY *speaks again.*

MARY If you get your price, what will you do with it?

JANET He won't get it.

JOHN *(to* **JANET***)* Do you suppose I'm going to sit down under his bullying?

JANET You've done it all your life.

JOHN Well, here's an end of it then.

JANET No one ever stands out against father for long – you know that – or else they get so knocked about they don't matter any more. *(She looks at* **MARY***, who has made an involuntary movement)* Oh, I don't mean he hits them – that's not his way.

JOHN Oh, don't exaggerate.

JANET Exaggerate – look at mother! You were too young – I remember— *(to* **MARY***)* You've been here nigh on three months. If you think you're going to change this house with your soft ways, you're mistaken. Nothing'll change us now – nothing. We're made that way – set – and we've got to live that way. *(Slowly)* You think you can make John do something. If ever he does it'll be for fear of father, not for love of you.

JOHN What do you mean? *(in a high voice)* If you think I'm going to give in—

JANET You've said that three times. I know you're going to give in.

JOHN Well, I'm not – so there.

JANET What will you do then?

JOHN That's my business. Curse Rutherford's! Curse it!

JANET *(to* **MARY***)* That's what he'll do. That's what he's been doing these five years. And what's come of it? He's dragged you into the life here – and Tony – that's all... I knew all the time you'd have to come in the end, to go under, like the rest of us.

MARY *(quickly)* No, no—

JANET Who's going to get you out of it? ...John? ...You're all getting excited about this metal. I don't know whether it's good or bad, but anyway it doesn't count. In a few days John'll make another row for us to sit round and listen to. In a few days more he'll threaten father to run away. He can't, because he's nothing separate from father. When he gives up his recipe, or whatever it is, it'll go to help Rutherford's – not you or me or anyone, just Rutherford's. And after a bit he'll forget about it – let it slide like the rest of us. We've all wanted things, one way and another, and we've let them slide. It's no good standing up against father.

JOHN Oh, who listens to you? Come along, Mary. *(Moving to the door)* Disagreeable old maid!

He goes out. **MARY** *stands in the same place looking at* **JANET**.

MARY Oh, Janet, no one's any right to be what he is – no one's any right.

JOHN *(calling from the hall)* Mollie! I want you. *(Irritably)* Mollie!

MARY Coming! *(she follows him)*

JANET *remains in the same attitude – her chin on her hands, staring sullenly before her. Suddenly she bows her face in her arms and begins to cry.* **MARTIN** *comes in from the kitchen on his way out. As he reaches the door leading to the hall, he sees her and stops.*

MARTIN *(in a whisper)* My lass!

She starts and gets up quickly.

JANET Martin! Martin!

He blunders over to her and takes her in his arms with a rough movement, holding her to him – kisses her with passion and without tenderness, and releases her suddenly. She goes to the fireplace, and leans her arms on the mantelpiece, her head on them – he turns away with his head bent. They stand so.

MARTIN *(as if the words were dragged from him)* Saturd'y night – he's away to Wickham – at the Tarn... Will ye come?

JANET Yes.

MARTIN *goes to the door at back. As he reaches it* **RUTHERFORD** *comes into the room with some papers in* *his hand. In crossing between the two, he stops suddenly as if some thought had struck him.*

MARTIN Goodnight, sir.

RUTHERFORD Goodnight. *(He stands looking at* **JANET** *till the outer door shuts)* Why don't you say goodnight to Martin? It 'ud be more civil – wouldn't it?

JANET I have said it.

Their eyes meet for a moment – she moves quickly to the door.

I'll tell Susan you're ready.

RUTHERFORD *is left alone. He stands in the middle of the room with his papers in his hand – motionless, save that he turns his head slowly to look at the door by which* **MARTIN** *has gone out.*

ACT TWO

It is about nine o'clock in the evening. The lamp is burning on the large table. Bedroom candlesticks are on the small table between the window and door.

RUTHERFORD *is sitting at his desk. He has been writing, and now sits staring in front of him with a heavy brooding face. He does not hear* **DICK** *as he comes in quietly and goes to the table to light his candle – then changes his mind, looks at his father, and comes to the fire to warm his hands. He looks, as usual, pale and tired.*

RUTHERFORD *becomes suddenly aware of his presence, upon which* **DICK** *speaks in a gentle, nervous tone.*

DICK I should rather like to speak to you, if you could spare me a minute.

RUTHERFORD What's the matter with you?

DICK The matter?

RUTHERFORD You're all wanting to speak to me nowadays – what's wrong with things? *(taking up his pen)* What's the bee in your bonnet?

DICK *(announcing his news)* I have been offered the senior curacy at St Jude's, Southport.

RUTHERFORD Well – have you taken it?

DICK *(disappointed)* I could not do so without your consent. That's what I want to speak to you about – if you could spare me a minute.

RUTHERFORD *(realising)* Ah! That means you're giving up your job here?

DICK Exactly.

RUTHERFORD Ah... Just as well, I dare say.

DICK You will naturally want to know my reasons for such a step. *(He waits for a reply and gets none)* In the first place, I have to consider my future. From that point of view there seems to be a chance of – of more success. And lately – I have had it in my mind for some time past – somehow my work among the people here hasn't met with the response I once hoped for... I have done my best – and it would be ungrateful to say that I had failed utterly when there are always the few who are pleased when I drop in... But the men are not encouraging.

RUTHERFORD I dare say not.

DICK I have done my best. Looking back on my three years here, I honestly cannot blame myself; and yet – failure is not the less bitter on that account.

RUTHERFORD *(almost kindly)* Well – perhaps a year or two at a Theological College wasn't the best of trainings for a raw hell like Grantley. It always beats me – whenever a man thinks it's his particular line to deal with humanity in the rough, he always goes to school like a bit of a lad to find out how to do it.

DICK Ah! You don't understand.

RUTHERFORD You mean I don't see things your way – well, that's not worth discussing. *(He goes back to his writing)*

DICK I have sometimes wondered if your not seeing things my way has had anything to do with my lack of success among your people. For they are your people.

RUTHERFORD What d'ye mean?

DICK *(sincerely!)* Not only the lack of religious example on your part – even some kind of Sunday observance would have helped – to be more in touch – but all through my ministry I have been conscious of your silent antagonism. Even in my active work – in talking to the men, in visiting their wives, in everything – I have always felt that dead weight against me, dragging me down, taking the heart out of all I do and say, even when I am most certain that I am right to do and say it. *(He ends rather breathlessly!)*

RUTHERFORD *(testily)* What the devil have you got hold of now?

DICK Perhaps I haven't made it clear what I mean.

RUTHERFORD *(deliberately)* I've never said a word against you or for you. And I've never heard a word against you or for you. Now! ...As for what you call your work, I don't know any more about it than a bairn, and I haven't time to learn. I should say that if you could keep the men out of the public houses and hammer a little decency into the women it might be a good thing. But I'm not an expert in your line.

DICK *(bold in his conviction)* Father – excuse me, but sometimes I think your point of view is perfectly deplorable.

RUTHERFORD Indeed! Frankly, I don't realise the importance of my point of view or of yours either. I got my work to do in the world – for the sake o' the argument, so have you – we do it or we don't do it. But what we think about it either way, doesn't matter.

DICK *(very earnestly)* It matters to God.

RUTHERFORD Does it. Now run along – I'm busy.

DICK This is all part of your resentment – your natural resentment – at my having taken up a different line to the one you intended for me.

RUTHERFORD Resentment – not a bit. Wear your collar-stud at the back if you like, it's all one to me. You can't make a silk purse out of a sow's ear – you were no good for my purpose, and there's an end. For the matter o' that, you might just as well never ha' been born – except that you give no trouble either way... Where's John?

DICK I don't know. His candle is here... I am still absolutely convinced that I chose the better part.

RUTHERFORD Probably. There are more ways than one of shirking life, and religion's one of them. If you want my blessing, here it is. As long as you respect my name and remember that I made a gentleman of ye, ye can go to the devil in your own way.

DICK Then I have your consent to accept St Jude's?

RUTHERFORD *(writing)* Aye. Just ring the bell before you go. I want my lamp.

> **DICK** *does so, depressed and disappointed. On his way to his candle he hesitates.*

DICK By the way – I'm forgetting – Mrs Henderson wants to see you.

RUTHERFORD And who is Mrs Henderson?

DICK William's mother.

RUTHERFORD William? ...The chap who's been pilfering my money? Oh, that matter's settled.

DICK Oh! ...Yes.

RUTHERFORD Goodnight. Did you ring?

DICK Yes. I rang. Goodnight. *(There is a silence, broken by the scratching of* RUTHERFORD*'s pen.* DICK *summons up his courage and speaks again)* I'm afraid I told Mrs Henderson she might call tonight.

RUTHERFORD Did ye now?

DICK Yes.

RUTHERFORD And what the devil did ye do that for, if one may enquire?

DICK She is one of my parishioners – in my district. She came to me – asked my help.

RUTHERFORD Told you the usual yarn, I suppose. More fool you, to be taken in by it. I can't see her.

DICK We don't know that it isn't true. The boy has been led astray by bad companions to bet and gamble. It's a regular gang – George Hammond's one, Fade's another.

RUTHERFORD I know them. Two of the worst characters and the best workers we've got.

DICK However that may be, the mother's in great grief, and I promised to intercede with you to give her son another chance.

RUTHERFORD Then you'd no business to promise anything of the kind. The lad's a young blackguard. Bless my soul – look at the head he's got on him! As bad an egg as you'll find in all your parish, and that's saying a good deal.

DICK I'm afraid it is – God help them. But—

A series of slow heavy knocks on the outer door are heard, ending with a belated single one.

I'm afraid that is Mrs Henderson.

RUTHERFORD *(going on with his writing)* Aye, it sounds like her hand. Been drowning her trouble, mebbee.

DICK *(after another knock)* Well. She's here.

RUTHERFORD You'd better go and tell her to go away again.

DICK Yes. *(He makes an undecided move towards the door; stops)* The woman ought to have a fair hearing.

RUTHERFORD *(losing patience)* Fair hearing! She's badgered Martin till he's had to turn her out, and on the top of it all you come blundering in with your talk of a fair hearing. *(He gets up and swings to the door, pushing* DICK *aside)* Here – let be.

DICK *(speaking with such earnestness that* RUTHERFORD *stops to look at him)* Father – one moment… Don't you think – don't you think it might be better to be friendly with her. To avoid unpleasantness? And gossip afterwards—

RUTHERFORD What? God help you for a fool, Richard. One would think I'd nothing to do but fash myself about this young blackguard and speak soft to his mother. *(He goes out into the hall and is heard opening the door)* Now, Mrs Henderson – you've come about your lad. You've had my answer.

MRS HENDERSON *is heard speaking apparently on the mat.*

MRS HENDERSON Oh, if you please, sir – if you could just see your way to sparin' me a minute I'd take it kindly, that would. And I come all the way from home on me two feet – and me a poor widder woman.

She drifts imperceptibly just inside the room. She is a large and powerful woman with a draggled skirt and a shawl over her head, and she is slightly drunk. RUTHERFORD *follows her in and stands by the open door, holding the handle.*

RUTHERFORD Well, then, out with it. What ha' ye got to say?

MRS HENDERSON It's my lad Bill as has been accused o' takin' your money—

RUTHERFORD Ten pounds.

MRS HENDERSON By Mr Martin, sir.

RUTHERFORD What then?

MRS HENDERSON And not another living soul near to say the truth of it.

RUTHERFORD Martin's my man, Mrs Henderson. What he does, he does under my orders. Besides, Martin and your son both say he took it. They've agreed about it.

MRS HENDERSON Aye, when he was scared out of his life he owned to it. I'm not denying he owned to it—

RUTHERFORD Oh, that's it, is it? He wants to go back on it? Why did he give up the money?

MRS HENDERSON He was that scared, sir, o' being sent to the gaol and losing his place and all, what wi' Mr Martin speaking that harsh to him, and all, and him a bit of a lad—

RUTHERFORD I see. In that case I owe him ten pounds?

MRS HENDERSON Eh?

RUTHERFORD I've took ten pounds off him, poor lad, all his honest savings mebbee. Goodnight, Mrs Henderson.

MRS HENDERSON Ah, Mr Rutherford, sir, don't 'ee be hard on us – don't 'ee now. We all got summat to be overlooked – every one on us when ye get down to it – and there's not a family harder working nor more respected in Grantley. Mr Richard here'll speak for us.

RUTHERFORD Speak for them, Richard.

DICK I... I do believe they are sincerely trying to do better.

RUTHERFORD Just so – better not rake up bygones. My time's short, Mrs Henderson, and you've no business to come up to the house at this time o' night, as you know well enough.

MRS HENDERSON Aye, sir, begging your pardon. I'm sure I'd be the last to intrude on you and the family if it warn't for—

RUTHERFORD I daresay. What did Martin say to you when you intruded into the glass-house?

MRS HENDERSON What did he say to me?

RUTHERFORD *(impatiently)* Aye.

MRS HENDERSON *(fervently)* Far be it from me to repeat what he did say. God forbid that I should dirty my mouth wi' the words that man turned on me! Before the men too, and half of 'em wi' their shirts off and me a decent woman. *(Violently)* 'Hawd yer whist,' I says to 'n. 'Hawd yer whist for a shameless—'

RUTHERFORD That'll do, that'll do – that's enough. You can take what Martin said from me. The matter's ended.

DICK *makes an appealing movement.*

Five years ago your son was caught stealing coppers out o' the men's coats – men poorer than himself. Don't forget that. I knew about it well enough. I gave him another chance because he was a young 'un, and because you ought to ha' taught him better.

MRS HENDERSON Me? Taught him better! That I should ever hear the like!

RUTHERFORD I gave him another chance. He made the most of it by robbing me the first time he thought he was safe not to be caught. Every man's got a right to go to the devil in his own way, as I've just been telling Mr Richard here, and your son Bill's old enough to choose his. I don't quarrel with him for that. But lads that get their fingers in my till are no use to me. And there's an end!

DICK Father! If you talk to her like this—

RUTHERFORD It's you that's brought her to hear me – you must take the consequences.

DICK No one is wholly bad – we have no right to say the lad is past hope, to condemn him utterly.

MRS HENDERSON Thank 'ee kindly, Mr Richard, sir – it's gospel truth every word of it. My son's as good a son as ever a lone woman had, but he's the spittin' image of his father, that easily led. And now to have him go wrong and all through keeping bad company and betting on the racing – just as he might ha' laid a bit on you, sir, in your young days and won his money too, sir, along o' your being sartain sure to win.

RUTHERFORD Well, I would have done my best to get him his money. But if I'd lost he'd ha' had to take his beating and pay up like a man and no whining about it. You take an interest in running?

MRS HENDERSON *(fervently)* Aye, sir, and always has done ever since I was a bit lass. And many's the Saturday me and my old man's gone down to the ground to see you run.

RUTHERFORD You don't happen to have heard who's won the quarter-of-a-mile at Broughton, do you?

DICK Father!

MRS HENDERSON I did hear as it was Dawson, sir, as I was passing.

RUTHERFORD Ah. Shepherd was overtrained. What time did he do – Dawson?

MRS HENDERSON I don't know, sir.

RUTHERFORD I made him a shade worse than six under at his trial. Shepherd should have been that.

DICK Father, please! Do let us talk this matter out seriously.

RUTHERFORD Seriously? What more?

DICK You see, it is as I said. I am sure Mrs Henderson will answer for her son's good conduct if you will consent to take him back – won't you, Mrs Henderson? Just this once. Your kindness may make all the difference, reform him altogether, who knows? He's had his lesson and I hate to preach, but – there is such a thing as repentence.

RUTHERFORD *(drily)* That's all right. You say what you think! And don't misunderstand me. I've no objection to Bill Henderson repenting, but I won't have him doing it in my Works, d'ye see? There's nothing spreads so quick as a nice soft feeling like that, and – who knows – we might have half-a-dozen other young blacklegs at the same game? Now, Mrs Henderson, go home like a sensible woman and send your lad away from Grantley. He'll soon find his feet if he's a mind to go straight. Keep him clear o' the pit towns – put him on a farm somewhere, where there aren't so many drinks going. And if I were you *(looking at her)*, why not go with him yourself?

MRS HENDERSON *(after a pause, suddenly truculent)* Me? Me leave Grantley? Me go to a place where I'm not respected and not a friend to speak for me? In Grantley I was born and in Grantley I'll live, like yourself. And beggin' your pardon, though you are the master, I'll joost take the liberty o' choosin' my own way.

RUTHERFORD Quite right – quite right. When you've lived and had your bairns and got drunk in a place you're apt to get attached to it. I'm that way myself. But it's just as well to change your drinks once in a while. It's only a friendly word of advice I'm giving you. Take it or leave it.

MRS HENDERSON *(bridling)* And so I will take it or leave it. Much obliged to 'ee.

RUTHERFORD And now go home, like a good woman.

MRS HENDERSON *(tossing her head with an unsteady curtsey)* And so I will, and a lot I got for my trouble – thank 'ee for nothing.

RUTHERFORD Thank me for not prosecuting your son, as I might ha' done.

MRS HENDERSON *(working herself up)* Prosecute! Prosecute my son! And why didn't ye do it? Ye darena' – that's why. You're feared o' folks talkin' – o' things said i' the court. And ye took and hided him and him a bit of a lad, and not a decent woman in Grantley but's crying shame on ye!

RUTHERFORD *(good-humouredly)* Now, Richard, this is where you come in. You brought her here.

MRS HENDERSON *(very shrill)* You let him off easy, did you? You give him another chance, did you? My lad could ha' had you up for assault – that's what he'd ha' done if he'd had a mind, and quite right too. It's him that's let you off, mind that. And you may thank your devil's luck you're not up afore the magistrate this next Assizes that ever is, and printed in the paper for all the countryside to mock at.

RUTHERFORD Go on, Richard. She's your parishioner. Turn her out.

MRS HENDERSON Him turn me out? A bit of a preaching bairn no stronger nor a linty – him with his good noos and his sojers-o'-Christ-arise! Whee was it up and ran away from old Lizzie Winter like a dawg wi' a kettle tied to his tail?

RUTHERFORD *(quietly without turning)* We'll have all your secrets in a minute. Are you going, Mrs Henderson?

MRS HENDERSON I'll go when it pleases me, and not afore!

RUTHERFORD Are you going—

He gets up and moves towards her in a threatening manner.

MRS HENDERSON *(retreating)* Lay hands on me! Lay hands on a helpless woman! I'll larn ye! I'll larn ye to come on me wi' yer high ways. Folks shall hear tell on it, that they shall, and a bit more besides. I'll larn ye, sure as I'm a living creature... I'll set the police on ye, as sure as I'm a living woman...

RUTHERFORD *(to* DICK, *contemptuously)* Hark to that – hark to it.

MRS HENDERSON You think yourself so grand wi' your big hoose, and your high ways. And your grandfather a potman like my own. You wi' your son that's the laughing-stock o' the parish and your daughter that goes wi' a working man ahint your back! And so goodnight to 'ee.

The outer door bangs violently. There is a pause.

DICK *speaks in a voice scarcely audible.*

DICK What was that? ...She said something – about Janet.

RUTHERFORD Well, what of it? *(impatiently)* Good God, man – don't stand staring there as if the house had fallen.

DICK *(shaking)* I told you to be careful – I warned you – I knew how it would be.

RUTHERFORD Warned me! You're fool enough to listen to what a drunken drab like that says!

DICK She's not the only one—

RUTHERFORD *(looking at him)* What d'ye mean? What's that?

DICK People are talking. I've – heard things… It isn't true – it can't be – it's too dreadful.

RUTHERFORD Heard things – what ha' ye heard?

DICK It isn't true.

RUTHERFORD Out with it.

DICK Lizzie Winter that time – called out something. I took no notice, of course… Three nights ago as I was coming home – past a public-house – the men were talking. I heard something then.

RUTHERFORD What was it you heard?

DICK There was his name, and Janet's. Then one of them George Hammond, I think it was – said something about having seen him on the road to the Tarn late one evening with a woman with a shawl over her head – Martin!

RUTHERFORD Martin!

DICK *(trying to reassure himself)* It's extremely unlikely that there is any truth in it at all. Why, he's been about ever since we were children. A servant, really. No one's ever thought of the possibility of such a thing. They will gossip, and one thing leads to another. It's easy to put two and two together and make five of them. That's all it is, we'll find. Why, even I can recall things I barely noticed at the time – things that might point to its being true – if it weren't so utterly impossible.

RUTHERFORD *(hoarsely)* Three nights gone. In this very room—

DICK What? *(running on again)* They've seen someone like Janet, and started the talk. It would be enough.

RUTHERFORD *(speaking to himself)* Under my roof—

DICK After dark on the road with a shawl – all women would look exactly alike… It's a pity he's taken the Tarn Cottage.

RUTHERFORD *(listening again)* Eh?

DICK I mean it's a pity it's happened just now.

RUTHERFORD A good mile from the Works.

DICK You can't see it from the village.

RUTHERFORD A good mile to walk, morn and night.

DICK No one goes there.

RUTHERFORD A lone place – a secret, he says to himself. Martin...

He stands by the table, his shoulders stooped, his face suddenly old. **DICK** *makes an involuntary movement towards him.*

DICK Father! Don't take it like that, for heaven's sake – don't look so broken.

RUTHERFORD Who's broken... *(he makes a sign to* **DICK** *not to come near)* Him to go against me. You're only a lad – you don't know. You don't know.

JOHN *comes into the room, evidently on his way to bed.*

JOHN *(idly)* Hullo! *(stops short, looking from one to the other)* What's the matter?

RUTHERFORD *(turning on him)* And what the devil do you want?

JOHN Want? – nothing... I thought you were talking about me, that's all.

RUTHERFORD About you, damn you – go to bed, the pair o' ye.

DICK Father—

RUTHERFORD Go to bed. There's men's work to be done here – you're best out o' the way. *(He goes to his desk and speaks down the tube)* Hulloh there – Hulloh!

DICK Wouldn't it be better to wait to talk things over? Here's John – you may be able to settle something – come to some arrangement.

RUTHERFORD Who's that? Gray – has Martin gone home? Martin! Tell him to come across at once – I want him. Aye – to the house – where else? Have you got it? Tell him at once.

JOHN *(suspicious)* I rather want a word with Martin myself. I think I'll stay.

RUTHERFORD You'll do as you're bid.

JOHN What do you want Martin for at this time of night?

RUTHERFORD That's my business.

JOHN About my metal—

RUTHERFORD Your metal! What the devil's your metal got to do with it? *(breaks off)*

JOHN *(excited)* Martin's got it. You know that. You're sending for him. Martin's honest – he won't tell you.

DICK Here's Janet.

JANET has come in in answer to the bell and stands by the door, sullen and indifferent, waiting for orders.

JANET Susan's gone to bed. *(As the silence continues, she looks round)* The bell rang.

DICK *(looking at* **RUTHERFORD***)* Some time ago. The lamp – father wanted his lamp.

She goes out.

JOHN *(rapidly)* It's no use going on like this, settling nothing either way. Sooner or later we've got to come to an understanding… *(***DICK** *makes a movement to stop him)* Oh, shut up, Dick!

He breaks off at a look from **RUTHERFORD**.

RUTHERFORD I want to have it clear. You heard what I said, three days past?

JOHN Yes, of course.

RUTHERFORD You still ask your price?

JOHN I told you – the thing's mine – I made it.

RUTHERFORD *(to* **JOHN***)* You've looked at it – fair and honest.

DICK Oh, what is the use of talking like this now? Father! you surely must see – under the circumstances – it isn't right – it isn't decent.

JOHN It's perfectly fair and just, what I ask. It benefits us both, the way I want it. You've made your bit. Rutherford's has served its purpose – and it's coming to an end – only you don't see it, Guv'nor. Oh, I know you're fond of the old place and all that

– it's only natural – but you can't live for ever – and I'm all right – if I get my price...

RUTHERFORD So much down for yourself – and the devil take Rutherford's.

JOHN You put it that way—

RUTHERFORD Yes or no?

JOHN Well – yes.

A knock is heard at the outer door.

DICK That's Martin, Father—

JOHN I'll stay and see him – I may as well.

RUTHERFORD Tomorrow – tomorrow I'll settle wi' ye.

JOHN looks at him in amazement; DICK makes a sign to him to come away; after a moment he does so.

JOHN *(turning as he reaches the door)* Thanks, Guv'nor – I thought you'd come to see things my way.

They go out.

RUTHERFORD Come in.

MARTIN comes in, cleaning his boots carefully on the mat – shuts the door after him and stands cap in hand. RUTHERFORD sits sunk in his chair, his hands gripping the arms.

MARTIN I came up as soon as I could get away.

Pause.

RUTHERFORD *(as if his lips were stiff)* You've stayed late.

MARTIN One o' the pots in Number Three Furnace ran down, and I had to stay and see her under way.

RUTHERFORD Sit down... Help yourself.

MARTIN Thank 'ee, sir. *(He comes to the table and pours out some whisky, then sits with his glass resting on his knee)* Winter's setting in early.

RUTHERFORD Ay—

MARTIN There's a heavy frost. The ground was hardening as I came along... They do say as Rayner's 'll be working again afore the week's out.

RUTHERFORD Given in – the men?

MARTIN Ay – the bad weather'll have helped it. Given a fine spell the men 'ud ha' hung on a while longer – but the cold makes 'em think o' the winter – turns the women and bairns agin them.

RUTHERFORD Ah!

MARTIN I thought you'd like to hear the coal 'ud be coming in all right, so I just went over to have a word wi' White the Agent this forenoon. *(He drinks, then as the silence continues, looks intently at* **RUTHERFORD***)* You sent for me?

JANET comes in carrying a reading-lamp. She halts for a moment on seeing **MARTIN***. He gets up awkwardly.*

(touching his forelock) Evenin'.

JANET Good evening.

She sets the lamp on the desk. **RUTHERFORD** *remains in the same position till she goes out, closing the door. There is a moment's silence, then* **MARTIN** *straightens himself, and they look at each other.*

MARTIN *(hoarsely)* You're wanting summat wi' me?

RUTHERFORD I want the recipe of Mr John's metal.

MARTIN *(between amazement and relief)* Eh?

RUTHERFORD You've got it.

MARTIN Ay—

RUTHERFORD Then give it me.

MARTIN I cannot do that, sir.

RUTHERFORD What d'ye mean?

MARTIN It's Mr John's own – what belongs to him – I canna do it.

RUTHERFORD On your high horse, eh, Martin? You can't do a dirty trick – you can't, eh?

MARTIN A dirty trick. Ye'll never be asking it of me – you never will—

RUTHERFORD I am asking it of ye. We've worked together five and twenty years, master and man. You know me. You know what there is'll stop me when I once make up my mind. I'm going to have this metal, d'ye understand. Whether Mr John gives it me or I take it, I'm going to have it.

MARTIN It's Mr John's own; if it's ever yourn, he must give it to ye himself. It's not for me to do it. He's found it, and it's his to do what he likes wi'. For me to go behind his back – I canna do it.

They look at each other; then **RUTHERFORD** *gets out of his chair and begins to pace up and down with his hands behind him. He speaks deliberately, with clumsy gestures and an air of driving straight to a goal.*

RUTHERFORD Sit down... Look how we stand. We've seven years' losing behind us, slow and sure. We've got the Bank that's poking its nose into this and that, putting a stop to everything that might put us on our legs again – because o' the risk... Rutherford's is going down – down – I got to pull her up somehow. There's one way out. If I can show the directors in plain working that I can cover the losses on the first year and make a profit on the second, I've got 'em for good and all.

MARTIN That's so – and Mr John'll see it, and ye'll come to terms—

RUTHERFORD Mr John's a fool. My son's a fool – I don't say it in anger. He's a fool because his mother made him one, bringing him up secret wi' books o' poetry and such-like trash – and when he'd grown a man and the time was come for me to take notice of him, he's turned agin me—

MARTIN He'll come roond – he's but a bit lad yet—

RUTHERFORD Turned agin me – agin me and all I done for him – all I worked to build up. He thinks it mighty clever to go working behind my back – the minute he gets the chance he's up on the hearthrug dictating his terms to me. He knows well enough I've counted on his coming after me. He's all I got since Richard went his ways – he's got me there... He wants his price, he says – his price for mucking around with a bit of a muffle furnace in his play-hours – that's what it comes to.

MARTIN Ay – but he's happened on a thing worth a bit.

RUTHERFORD Luck! Luck! What's he done for it? How long has he worked for it – tell me that – an hour here and a bit there – and he's got it! I've slaved my life long, and what have I got for it? Toil and weariness. That's what I got – bad luck on bad luck battering on me – seven years of it. And the worst bit I've had yet is that when it turns it's put into my son's hands to give me or not, if you please, as if he was a lord.

MARTIN He'll come roond – lads has their notions – we all want to have things for ourselves when we're young, all on us—

RUTHERFORD Want – want – lad's talk! What business has he to want when there's Rutherford's going to the dogs?

MARTIN That canna be, it canna – he'll have to see different.

RUTHERFORD He won't see different.

MARTIN He'll learn.

RUTHERFORD When it's too late. Look here, Martin, we can't go on – you know that as well as I do – leastways you've suspected it. Ten years more as things are'll see us out. Done with! Mr John's made this metal – a thing, I take your word for it, that's worth a fortune. And we're going to sit by and watch him fooling it away – selling it for a song to Miles or Jarvis, that we could break tomorrow if we had half a chance. And they'll make on it, make on it – while Rutherford's 'll grub on as we've been grubbing for the last seven years. I'm speaking plain now – I'm saying what I wouldn't say to another living man. We can't go on. You've been with me through it all. You've seen me do it. You've seen the drag and the struggle of it – the days when I've nigh thrown up the sponge for very weariness – the bit o' brightness that made me go on – the times when I've stood up to the Board, sick in the heart of me, with nothing but my will to turn 'em this way or that. And at the end of it – I come up against this – a bit o' foolishness – just foolishness – and all that I done'll break on that – just that.

MARTIN Nay – nay—

RUTHERFORD I'm getting old, they say – old – there's new ways in the trade, they say. And in their hearts they see me, out of it – out o' the place I built afore they learnt their letters, many of 'em—

MARTIN That'll never be.

RUTHERFORD Why not – when you've got but to put your hand in your pocket to save the place and you don't do it. You're with them – you're with the money-grubbing little souls that can't see beyond the next shilling they put in their pockets, that's content to wring the old place dry, then leave it to the rats – you're with a half-broke puppy like Mr John that wants to grab his bit for himself and clear out. Twenty-five years...and you go snivelling about what Mr John thinks of ye – what's right for you to do. Everybody for himself – his pocket or his soul, it's all one. And Rutherford's loses her chance through the lot o' ye. Blind fools!

MARTIN You blame me – you put me i' the wrong. It's like as if I'd have to watch the old place going down year by year, and have it on my mind that I might ha' saved her. But Mr John's got his rights.

RUTHERFORD You think I'm getting this metal for myself against Mr John?

MARTIN I'm loth to say it.

RUTHERFORD Answer me—

MARTIN Mr John'll see it that way.

RUTHERFORD Stealing like, out o' his pocket into mine. When men steal, Martin, they do it to gain something. If I steal this, what'll I gain by it? If I make money, what'll I buy with it? Pleasure mebbee? Children to come after me – glad o' what I done? Tell me anything in the wide world that'd bring me joy, and I'll swear to you never to touch it.

MARTIN If you think what you're saying it's a weary life you got to face.

RUTHERFORD If you give it to me, what'll you gain by it? Not a farthing shall you ever have from me – no more than I get myself.

MARTIN And what'll Mr John get for it?

RUTHERFORD Rutherford's – when I'm gone. *(After a silence)* He'll thank you in ten years – he'll come to laugh at himself – him and his price. He'll see the Big Thing one day mebbee, like what I've done. He'll see that it was no more his to keep than 'twas yours to give nor mine to take... It's Rutherford's... Will you give it to me?

MARTIN *(facing him)* If I thought that we'd make a farthing out of it, either on us—

RUTHERFORD Will ye give it me—

MARTIN *stands looking at him, then slowly begins to feel in his pockets.*

Got it – on you?

MARTIN *(taking out a pocket-book)* He'll never forgi' me, Mr John won't – never i' this world... It should be somewheres. He'll turn agin me – it'll be as if I stole it.

RUTHERFORD Got it?

MARTIN Nay, I mun' ha' left it up hame. Ay, I call to mind, now – I locked it away to keep it safe.

RUTHERFORD Can ye no' remember it? Think, man – think!

MARTIN Nay, I canna be sure. I canna call the quantities to mind.

RUTHERFORD *(violently)* Think – think – you must know!

MARTIN *(wonderingly)* I can give it 'ee first thing i' the morning.

RUTHERFORD I want it tonight... No, no – leave it – you might get it wrong – better make sure – bring it up in the morning. Goodnight to 'ee – goodnight. And remember – I take your word to bring it – no going back, mind ye—

MARTIN Nay, nay. *(Turning to go)* I doubt if Mr John'll ever see it in the way you do. If you could mebbee explain a bit when he hears tell of it – put in a word for me, belike—

RUTHERFORD I'm to bed.

MARTIN I take shame to be doing it now.

RUTHERFORD Off wi' ye – off wi' ye – wi' your conscience so delicate and tender. Keep your hands clean, or don't let any one see them dirty – it'll do as well.

MARTIN He worked it out along o' me. Every time it changed he come running to show me like a bairn wi' a new toy.

RUTHERFORD It's for Rutherford's...

MARTIN Ay, for Rutherford's – Goodnight, sir.

He goes out.

After a pause, **JANET** *comes in to put things straight for the night. She goes into the hall and is heard putting the chain on the outer door – comes back, locking the inner door – then takes the decanter from the tray and locks it in the sideboard, laying the key on the desk.*

RUTHERFORD *stands on the hearthrug. As she takes up the tray he speaks.*

RUTHERFORD How long has this been going on atween you and Martin?

She puts the tray down and stands staring at him with a white face.

JANET How long?

RUTHERFORD Answer me.

JANET September – about when Mary and Tony came.

There is a long silence. When it becomes unbearable she speaks again.

What are you going to do? *(he makes no answer)* You must tell me what you're going to do?

RUTHERFORD Keep my hands off ye.

JANET You've had him here.

RUTHERFORD That's my business.

JANET *(speaking in a low voice as if she were repeating a lesson)* It wasn't his fault. It was me. He didn't come after me I went after him.

RUTHERFORD Feel – proud o' yourself?

JANET You can't punish him for what isn't his fault. If you've got to punish anyone, it's me...

RUTHERFORD How far's it gone?

JANET *(after a pause)* Right at first. I made up my mind that if you ever found out, I'd go right away, to put things straight. *(She goes on presently in the same toneless voice)* He wanted to tell you at the first. But I knew it would be no use. And once we'd spoken – every time was just a little more. So we let it slide... It was I said not to tell you.

RUTHERFORD Martin...that I trusted as I trust myself.

JANET I'll give him up.

RUTHERFORD You can't give him back to me. He was a straight man. What's the good of him now? You've dragged the man's heart out of him with your damned woman's ways.

She looks at him.

JANET You haven't turned him away – you couldn't do that!

RUTHERFORD That's my business.

JANET You couldn't do that – not Martin...

RUTHERFORD Leave it – leave it... Martin's my servant, that I pay wages to I made a name for my children – a name respected in all the countryside – and you go with a workingman. Tomorrow you leave my house. D'ye understand. I'll have no light ways under my roof. No one shall say I winked at it. You can bide the night. Tomorrow when I come in, I'm to find ye gone... Your name shan't be spoke in my house...never again.

JANET Yes. *(she stands looking down at the table, then slowly moves to go, her feet dragging – stops for a moment and says in a final tone, almost with a sigh of relief)* Then there'll be no need for anybody to know it was Martin—

RUTHERFORD No need to know. Lord, you drive me crazy! With all Grantley telling the story – my name in every public-house.

JANET When I'm gone. *(Looking up)* What did you say?

RUTHERFORD It's all over the place by now. Richard's heard it – your own brother... You've been running out o' night, I suppose. Somebody's seen.

JANET What's Dick heard?

RUTHERFORD What men say about women like you. They got a word.

JANET The men... O God!

RUTHERFORD Ay – you say that now the thing's done – you'll whine and cry out now you done your worst agin me.

JANET Let me be.

RUTHERFORD You're going to put things straight, are ye you're going to walk out comfortable wi' your head up and your fine talk.

JANET I'm ready to stand by it.

RUTHERFORD It's not you that's got to stand by it – it's me! What ha' you got to lose? Yourself, if you've a mind to. That's all. It's me that's to be the laughing-stock – the Master whose daughter goes wi' a working-man like any Jenny i' the place—

JANET Oh! You stand there! To drive me mad—

RUTHERFORD That'll do – that'll do. I've heard enough. You've confessed, and there's an end.

JANET Confessed? As if I'd stolen something. *(Brokenly)* You put it all on to me, every bit o' the wrong.

RUTHERFORD Ah, you'll set to and throw the blame on Martin now. I thought we'd come to it.

JANET No, no. I've taken that. But...you make no excuse... You think of this that I've done separate from all the rest – from all the years I done as you bid me, lived as you bid me.

RUTHERFORD What's that to do wi' it? I'm your father! I work for 'ee... I give 'ee food and clothes for your back! I got a right to be obeyed – I got a right to have my children live respectable in the station where I put them. You gone wrong. That's what you done. And you try to bring it up against me because I set you up i' the world. Go to bed!

JANET Oh, you've no pity... *(she makes a movement to go, then turns again as if for a moment)* I was thirty-six. Gone sour. Nobody'd ever come after me. Not even when I was young. You took care o' that. Half of my life was gone, well-nigh all of it that mattered... What have I had of it, afore I go back to the dark? What have I had of it? Tell me that. Tell me!

RUTHERFORD Where's the man as 'ud want you wi' your sulky ways?

JANET I've sat and sewed – gone for a walk – seen to the meals – every day – every day... That's what you've given me to be my life – just that!

RUTHERFORD Talk, talk, talk! Fine words to cover up the shame and disgrace you brought on me—

JANET On you?

RUTHERFORD Where'd you ha' been if I hadn't set you up?

JANET Down in the village – in amongst it, with the other women – in a cottage – happy mebbee.

RUTHERFORD *(angrily)* I brought you up for a lady as idle as you please – you might ha' sat wi' your hands afore you from morn till night if ye'd had a mind to.

JANET Me a lady? What do ladies think about, sitting the day long with their hands before them? What have they in their idle hearts?

RUTHERFORD What more did you want, in God's name?

JANET Oh, what more! The women down there know what I wanted...with their bairns wrapped in their shawls and their men to come home at night time. I've envied them – envied them their pain, their poorness – the very times they hadn't bread. Theirs isn't the dead empty house, the blank o' the moors; they got something to fight, something to be feared of. They got life, those women we send cans o' soup to out o' pity when their bairns are born. Me a lady! With work for a man in my hands, passion for a man in my heart! I'm common – common.

RUTHERFORD It's a lie! I've risen up. You can't go back on it – my children can't go back.

JANET Who's risen – which of us?

RUTHERFORD You say that because you've shamed yourself, and you're jealous o' them that keep decent like gentlefolk—

JANET Dick – that every one laughs at? John – with his manners?

RUTHERFORD Whisht wi' your wicked tongue!

JANET Who's Mary? A little common work-girl – no real gentleman would ha' looked at... You think you've made us different by keeping from the people here. We're just the same as they are! Ask the men that work for you – ask their wives that curtsey to us in the road. Do you think they don't know the difference? We're just the same as they are common, every one of us. It's in our blood, in our hands and faces; and when we marry, we marry common—

RUTHERFORD Marry! Common or not, nobody's married you that I can see—

JANET Leave that – don't you say it!

RUTHERFORD It's the truth, more shame to 'ee.

JANET (*passionately*) Martin loves me honest. Don't you come near! Don't you touch that! ...You think I'm sorry you've found out – you think you've done for me when you use shameful words on me and turn me out o' your house.

You've let me out o' gaol! Whatever happens to me now, I shan't go on living as I lived here. Whatever Martin's done, he's taken me from you. You've ruined my life, you with your getting on. I've loved in wretchedness, all the joy I ever had made wicked by the fear o' you... (*Wildly*) Who are you? Who are you? A man – a man that's taken power to himself, power to gather people to him and use them as he wills – a man that'd take the blood of life itself and put it into the Works – into Rutherford's. And what ha' you got by it – what? You've got Dick, that you've bullied till he's a fool – John, that's waiting for the time when he can sell what you've done – and you got me – me to take your boots off at night – to well-nigh wish you dead when I had to touch you... Now! ...Now you know!

ACT THREE

It is about eleven o'clock on the following morning. **JANET** *is sitting at the table with a shawl about her shoulders talking in low tones to* **MARY**, *who is opposite.*

JANET *(after a pause)* You mean that you guessed?

MARY Yes.

JANET You knew all the time, and you didn't tell? Not even John?

MARY Why should I tell him?

JANET I would ha' told Martin if it had been you.

MARY Not John.

JANET It was good of you. You've always been better to me than I've been to you.

MARY What are you going to do?

JANET He says I'm to go. He's to come in and find me gone, and no one's to speak of me any more. Not John, nor Dick, nor Aunt Ann – I'm never to set foot in this room again. Never to lock up and give him the keys last thing. Never to sit the long afternoon through in the window, till the furnaces are bright in the dark. I've done what women are shamed for doing – and all the night I've barely slept for the hope in my heart.

MARY Hope?

JANET Of things coming. I had a dream – a dream that I was in a place wi' flowers, in the summer-time, white and thick like they never grow on the moor – but it was the moor – a place near Martin's cottage. And I dreamt that he came to me with the look he had when I was a little lass, with his head up and the lie gone out of his eyes. All the time I knew I was on my bed in my room here – but it was like as if sweetness poured into me, spreading and covering me like the water in the tarn when the rains are heavy in the fells.

MARY Is Mr Rutherford very angry?

JANET He won't never hear my name again. Oh, last night I said things to him, when he blamed me so – things he can't never forget. I was wild – mad with the bitterness of it. He made it all ugly with the things he said. I told him what I never looked to tell him, though I'd had it in my heart all these years. All the time I was speaking I was dead with shame that he should know, and I had to go on. But afterwards – it was as I'd slipped a burden, and I was glad he knew, glad that Dick heard it in the street, glad that he sneaked of me behind my back – glad! For, when I'd got over the terror of it, it came to me that this was what we'd been making for ever since you came without knowing it, that we were to win through to happiness after all, Martin and I, and everything come right. Because I've doubted. Men's lives are different to ours. And sometimes, when we've stolen together, and afterwards I've seen his face and the sadness of it, I've wondered what I had to give him that could count against what he'd lost. And I've gone with black despair on me, and the fear of losing him. You don't know what that fear's like you don't know – to love him with all my heart, so that there was no one else in the world but him – and to know that any day, any minute, it might all slip away from me, and me be helpless to hold it – helpless!

MARY But that's done with now.

JANET Yes! That's why I dreamt of him so last night. It was as if all that was best in me was in that dream – what I was as a bairn, and what I'm going to be. He couldn't help but love me. It was a message – I couldn't have thought of it by myself. It's something that's come to me, here. *(Putting her hands on her breast)* Part of me.

MARY *looks at her with a new understanding. After a pause she speaks again, very gently.*

MARY Where are you going when Martin comes for you?

JANET I don't know yet. He'll say what to do.

MARY Have you got your things ready?

JANET *(as if she scarcely heard)* Yes.

MARY I could see to them for you.

JANET They're all ready. I put them together early in the box mother had. *(She breaks off, listening)*

MARY Janet, if ever the time should be when you want help – and it does happen sometimes even to people who are very happy – remember that I'll come when you ask me – always.

JANET He's coming now! *(She sits listening, her eyes bright.* MARY *goes out quietly closing the door)*

MARTIN *comes in from the hall.*

(Very tenderly) Martin! *(He stands in the doorway, his cap in his hands, his head bent. He looks spent, broken, and at the sight of him the hope dies slowly out of her face)*

MARTIN Is Mr John about?

JANET I don't know.

MARTIN I mun see 'n. I got summat to say to 'n.

JANET He's down at the Works mebbee—

MARTIN I canna seek him there – I got summat to say to 'n.

JANET You could give a message.

MARTIN Nay. It's summat that's got to be said to his face – like a man.

JANET Have you nothing to say to me, Martin – to my face like a man?

MARTIN What should there be to say betwixt you and me? It's all said long since.

JANET He's turned you away? *(He raises his eyes and looks at her for the first time)*

MARTIN Ay. You've said it. What I've been trying to tell myself these three months past. Turned away I am, sure enough. Twenty-five year. And in a minute it's broke. Wi' two words.

JANET He'll call you back. He can't do without you, Martin. He's done it in anger like he was last night. He'll call you back.

MARTIN He never calls no one back. He's a just man, and he's in the right of it. Anger – there's no anger in a face that's twisting like a bairn's – white as if it was drained o' the blood. There's no anger in a man that stands still where he is, when he might ha' struck and killed and still been i' the right.

JANET *gets up slowly and goes to the fire.*

JANET Come and get warm by the fire. It's a bitter cold morning. Come and get warm.

He moves slowly across and sits on the settle. She kneels beside him, takes his hands and begins to rub them.

(as if he were a child) Your hands are as cold, as cold – like frozen. It's all fresh and new to you now, my dear, the surprise of it. It'll pass – and by-and-by you'll forget it – be glad, mebbee. Did you get your breakfast?

MARTIN Ay.

JANET What have you been doing – since?

MARTIN Walking – walking. Up on the fell I been – trying to get it clear—

JANET On the fell, in such weather! That's why you're so white and weary. You should have come to me, my honey – you should ha' come straight to me. I would ha' helped you, my dear – out of my love for 'ee.

MARTIN There's no help.

JANET You say that now because your heart's cold with the trouble. But it'll warm again – it'll warm again, I'll warm it – out of my own heart, Martin – my heart that can't be made cold, not if he killed me. Why, last night he was just the same with me as he's been with you. I know it all – there's nothing you feel that I don't know. We'll face it together, you and me, equal – and by-and-by it'll be different. What we done was for love – people give up everything for love, Martin; every day they say there's someone in the world that does it. Don't 'ee take on so – don't 'ee.

MARTIN Twenty-five year—

JANET Don't 'ee, my dear.

MARTIN *(brokenly)* I'd rather ha' died than he turn me away. I'd ha' lost everything in the world to know that I was true to 'n, like I was till you looked at me wi' the love in your face.

JANET Everything in the world... I gave you joy – joy for the toil he gave you, softness for his hardness.

MARTIN *(without bitterness)* Ay, you were ready. And you gave the bitter with the sweet. Every time there was him to face, wi' a heart like lead.

JANET It was a power – a power that came, stronger than us both.

MARTIN You give me the word.

JANET You took away my strength. *(There is a silence. He sits looking dully at the fire)* Anyone might think me light. It isn't true. I never had anyone but you, never. All my life I've been alone. When I was a little lass I wasn't allowed to play with the other bairns, and I used to make signs to tell them I wanted to. You'd never have known I loved you if I hadn't given you the word – and all our happiness, all that's been between us, we'd never have had it – gone through our lives seeing each other, speaking words that didn't matter, and grown old and never known what was sleeping in our hearts under the dullness. I wasn't light. It was only that I couldn't be shamed for you.

MARTIN Nay, nay, it was a great love ye gave me – you in your grand hoose wi' your delicate ways. But it's broke me.

JANET But – it's just the same with us. Just the same as ever it was.

MARTIN Ay. But there's no mending, wi' the likes o' him.

JANET What's there to mend? What's there to mend except what's bound you like a slave all the years? You're free – free for the first time since you were a lad mebbee – to make a fresh start.

MARTIN A fresh start? Wi' treachery and a lyin' tongue behind me?

JANET With our love that nothing can break. Oh, my dear, I'll help 'ee. Morning, noon, and night I'll work for 'ee, comfort 'ee. We'll go away from it all, you and me together. We'll go to the south, where no one's heard tell of Rutherford's or any of us. I'll love 'ee so. I'll blind your eyes wi' love so that you can't look back.

MARTIN *(looking up)* Ay. There's that.

JANET We'll begin again. We'll be happy – happy. You and me, free in the world! All the time that's been'll be just like a dream that's past, a waiting time afore we found each other – the long winter afore the flowers come out white and thick on the moors—

MARTIN He'll be lookin' to me to right ye. He'll be lookin' for that.

JANET To right me?

MARTIN Whatever's been, they munna say his daughter wasn't made an honest woman of. He'll be lookin' for that.

There is a silence. She draws back slowly, dropping her hands.

JANET What's he to do with it?

He looks at her, not understanding.

Father – what's he to do with it?

MARTIN It's for him to say – the Master.

JANET Master!

MARTIN What's come to ye, lass?

JANET It's time you left off doing things because of him. You're a free man. He's not your master any more.

MARTIN What's wrong wi' ye?

JANET You'll right me because of him. You'll make an honest woman of me because he's looking for it. He can't make you do as he bids you now. He's turned you away. He's not your master any more. He's turned you away.

MARTIN Whisht – whisht. *(He sinks his head in his hands)* Nay, but it's true. I'll never do his work again. But I done it too long to change – too long.

JANET He's done with you – that's how much he cares. I wouldn't ha' let you go, not if you'd wronged me.

MARTIN Twenty-five years ago he took me from nothing. Set me where I could work my way up – woke the lad's love in me till I would ha' died for him – willing. It's too long to change.

JANET *(passionately)* No – no.

MARTIN I'll never do his work no more; but it's like as if he'd be my master just the same – till I die—

JANET No, no, not that! You mustn't think like that! You think he's great because you've seen him at the Works with the men – everybody doing as he bids them. He isn't great – he's hard and cruel – cruel as death.

MARTIN What's took you to talk so wild?

JANET *(holding him)* Listen, Martin. Listen to me. You've worked all your life for him, ever since you were a little lad. Early and late you've been at the Works – working – working for him.

MARTIN Gladly!

JANET Now and then he gie you a kind word – when you were wearied out mebbee – and your thoughts might ha' turned to what other men's lives were, wi' time for rest and pleasure. You didn't see through him, you wi' your big heart, Martin. You were too near to see, like I was till Mary came. You worked gladly, mebbee – but all the time your life was going into Rutherford's – your manhood into the place he's built. He's had you, Martin – like he's had me, and all of us. We used to say he was hard and ill-tempered. Bad to do with in the house – we fell silent when he came in – we couldn't see for the little things – we couldn't see the years passing because of the days. And all the time it was our lives he was taking bit by bit – our lives that we'll never get back.

MARTIN What's got ye to talk so wild?

He moves from her as she talks and clings to him.

JANET Now's our chance at last! He's turned us both away, me as well as you. We two he's sent out into the world together. Free. He's done it himself, of his own will. It's ours to take, Martin – our happiness. We'll get it in spite of him. He'd kill it if he could.

MARTIN Whisht, whisht! You talk wild!

JANET Kill it, kill it! He's gone nigh to it as it is. *(As he makes a movement to rise)* Martin, Martin, I love 'ee. I'm old – with the lines on my face – but it's him that's made me so. I'm bitter-tongued and sharp – it's him that's killed the sweetness in me, starved it till it died. He's taken what should have been yours to have your joy of. Stolen it – remember that – and say he's in the right! Say it when you wish me young and bonny. Say it as I shall when I look in your face for the love that can't wake for me.

MARTIN Bide still, bide still!

JANET I wouldn't ha' turned against you, not if you'd nigh killed me – and you set his love up against mine! Martin!

He gets up, not roughly, but very wearily, and moves away from her.

MARTIN It bain't the time, it bain't the time. I been a bad servant. Faithless. We can twist words like we done all along to make it seem different, but there it stands. Leave him, when you talk to me. Leave him... Mebbee he's had his mind full of a big work when you've took a spite of him.

JANET Ah!

MARTIN Womenfolk has their fancies, and mebbee they don't know the harshness that's in the heart of every man that fights his way i' the world when he comes into the four walls of his bit boose of a night and sees the littleness of it. *(Standing by the table)* I'm a plain man with no book larning, and mebbee I don't see far. But I've watched the Master year in year out, and I never seed him do a thing, nor say a thing, that he warn't in the right of. And there's not a man among them that can say different. *(Taking up his cap)* I'll be seekin' Mr John.

JANET *(speaks in a dull, toneless voice, kneeling where he left her)* He says I have to be gone by the time he comes in. Where am I to go to?

He turns to look at her with a puzzled face.

MARTIN Ay. There's that.

JANET Where am I to go?

MARTIN It would be best to go a bit away – where ye wouldna' be seen for a while.

JANET Where's a place – far enough?

MARTIN There's Horkesley – up the line. Or Hillgarth yonder. He's not likely to be knawed thereaboots.

JANET I haven't any money.

MARTIN *slowly counts out some coins on the table.*

MARTIN It'll be a hard life for you, and you not used to it. Work early and late – wi' a bairn mebbee. Bitter cold i' the winter mornings wi' the fire to light and the breakfast to get, and you not used to it; we mun just bide it, the pair on us. Make the best of it. I've saved two hundred pounds. There'll be summat to get along whilst I look for a job. Afterwards we mun just bide it.

There is a silence.

JANET *(without bitterness)* Take up your money.

MARTIN *(puzzled)* It's for you, lass.

JANET Take up your money. I'll have no need of it.

After a moment he picks it up and returns it to his pocket.

(still kneeling) After all, you'd give the world to ha' been true to him – you'd give me, that you said was the world.

He'd have you back if it wasn't for me. He needs you for the Works. If I was out of it there'd be no more reason – you'd go back, and people would think it all a mistake about you and me. Gossip. After a bit he'd forget and be the same. Because he needs you for the Works. Men forgive men easy where it's a woman, they say, and you could blame me, the pair of you. Me that gave you the word.

MARY *comes in hurriedly.*

MARY John's coming. He's coming across from the Works.

MARTIN *turns to face the door.* **JANET** *does not move.* **JOHN** *comes in excited and nervous.*

JOHN *(awkwardly)* Hullo! *(He looks at* **JANET** *and speaks to* **MARTIN***)* What are you here for?

MARTIN Mr John – I summat to say to you – summat I must say afore I go.

JOHN You'd better keep quiet, I should think. Oh, I know! I've been with the Guv'nor, and he's told me plain enough. You'd better keep quiet.

MARY John, you must listen.

JOHN I tell you I know! The less we talk about it the better; I should think you would see that – the whole beastly, disreputable business. I can't stay – I can't talk calmly, if you can – I'm better out of it. *(He makes for the door.* **MARTIN** *stops him)*

MARTIN Mr John... You been wi' the Master. What was it he told you – plain enough?

JOHN *(significantly)* What was it!

MARTIN Did he tell you he'd got your metal?

JOHN *looks at him.*

JOHN Are you mad?

MARTIN I've give it him – I took it him this morning, and when he got it safe he turned me away. That's what I got to say.

JOHN *(sharply)* I don't believe it! You can't have! You haven't got the quantities!

MARTIN The paper I took the last trial we made—

JOHN *(his voice high-pitched with excitement)* Don't – don't play the fool.

MARTIN I'm speaking God's truth, and you'd best take it. Yesterday night he sent for me – and I give it him, because he asked me for it. He was i' the right, yesterday night – I don't call to mind how. And just now I give it him. That's what I got to say.

JOHN *stands staring at him speechless.* **MARTIN** *having said what he came to say, turns to go.* **MARY**, *suddenly realising what it all means, makes an involuntary movement to stop him.*

MARY Martin! You've given the recipe to Mr Rutherford! He's got it – he'll take the money from it! ...You're sure of what you say, Martin? You haven't made a mistake?

MARTIN Mistake?

MARY You may have got it wrong – the quantities, or whatever it is. It all depends on that, doesn't it? The least slip would put it all wrong, wouldn't it?

MARTIN *(tired out and dull)* There's no mistake.

MARY *(with a despairing movement)* Oh! You don't know what you've done!

JOHN *(almost in tears)* He knows well enough – you knew well enough. You're a thief – you're as bad as he is – you two behind my back. It was mine – the only chance I had. Damn him! Damn him! You've done for yourself, that's one thing – you're done for! You'll not get anything out of it now, not a farthing. He's twisted you round his finger, making you think you'd have the pickings, has he? And then thrown you out into the street for a fool and worse. You're done for! ...You've worked with me, seen it grow. I never thought but to trust you as I trusted myself – and you give it away thinking to make a bit behind my back! You'll not get a farthing now – not a farthing – you're done for.

MARTIN Hard words, Mr John, from you to me. But I done it, and I mun bide by it.

JOHN Oh, clear out – don't talk to me. By heaven! I'll be even with him yet.

MARTIN I done it – but it bain't true what you think, that I looked to make a bit. I give it to him, but I had no thought o' gain by what I done... It's past me – it's all past me – I canna call it to mind, nor see it plain. But I know one thing, that I never thought to make a penny. *(Suddenly remembering)* It was for Rutherford's – that's what he said – I mind it now. He said, for Rutherford's – and I seed it yesterday night. It was as clear as day – yesterday night.

No one answers. After a moment he goes out.

As the outer door closes **JOHN** *suddenly goes to* **RUTHERFORD**'s *desk and begins pulling out drawers as if searching for something.*

MARY *(watching him)* What are you doing?

JOHN Where's the key, curse it!

MARY *(sharply)* You can't do that!

JOHN Do what? I'm going to get even.

MARY Not money! You can't take his money!

JOHN *(unlocking the cash box)* Just be quiet, will you? He's taken all I have. *(He empties the money out on to the desk; his hands shaking)* Fifteen – twenty – twenty-three. And it's twenty-three thousand he owes me more like, that he's stolen. Is there any more – a sixpence I've missed, that'll help to put us even? Twenty-three quid – curse him! And he stood and talked to me not an hour ago, and all the time he knew! He's mean, that's what he is – mean and petty-minded. No one else could have done it – to go and get at Martin behind my back because he knew I was going to be one too many for him.

MARY *(imploringly)* Put it back! Oh, put it back!

JOHN Oh, shut up, Mollie.

MARY Don't take it, John.

JOHN I tell you it's mine, by right – you don't understand... How am I to get along if I don't?

MARY You've not got to do this, John – for Tony's sake. I don't care what he's done to you – you've not got to do it.

JOHN Don't make a tragedy out of nothing. It's plain common sense! *(Angrily)* And don't look at me as if I were stealing. It's mine, I tell you. I only wish there were a few thousands – I'd take them!

MARY John, listen to me. I've never seriously asked you to do anything for me in my life. Just this once – I ask you to put that money back.

JOHN My dear girl, don't be so foolish—

MARY *(compelling him to listen to her)* Listen! You're Tony's father! I can't help it if you think I'm making a tragedy out of what seems to you a simple thing. One day he'll know – someone'll tell him that you stole money – well then, that you took money that wasn't yours, because you thought you had the right to it. What will it be like for him? Try and realise – we've no right to live as we like – we've had our day together, you and I – but it's past, and we know it. He's what matters now – and we've got to live decently for him – keep straight for him—

JOHN *(answering her like an angry child)* Then do it! I've had enough – I'm sick of it.

JANET, who all this time has been kneeling where MARTIN left her, gets up suddenly, stumbling forward as if she were blind. The other two stop involuntarily and watch her as she makes for the door, dragging her shawl over her head. As the outer door shuts on her, MARY with a half-cry makes a movement to follow her.

MARY Janet!

JOHN Oh, let her be!

MARY *(facing the door)* Where's she going to?

JOHN I'm not going to argue – I've done that too long – listening to first one and then another of you. What's come of it? You wouldn't let me go out and sell the thing while it was still mine to sell. I might have been a rich man if I'd been let to go my own way! You were always dragging me back, everything I did – with your talk. Tony – you're perpetually cramming him down my throat, till I'm sick of the very name of the poor little beggar. How much better off is he for your interfering? Give up this and give up that – I've lost everything I ever had by doing as you said. Anybody would have bought it, anybody! and made a fortune out of it – and there it is, lost! Gone into Rutherford's, like everything else. Damn the place! Damn it! Oh, let him wait! I'll be even with him. I came back once because I was a soft fool – this time I'll starve sooner.

MARY You're going away?

JOHN Yes, I'm going for good and all.

She stands looking at him.

MARY Where are you going to?

JOHN London – anywhere. Canada, probably – that's the place to strike out on your own—

MARY You mean to work then?

JOHN *(impatiently)* Of course. We can't live for ever on twenty-three quid.

MARY What are you going to work at?

JOHN Anything – as long as I show him—

MARY But what – what?

JOHN Oh, there'll be something. Damn it, Mary, what right have you to catechise?

MARY Don't, please. I'm not catechising; I want to know. It's a question of living. What are you going to do when you've spent what you've got?

JOHN *(trying not to look shamefaced as he makes the suggestion)* You could go back to Mason's for a bit – they'd be glad enough to have you.

MARY Go back?

JOHN *(resentfully)* Well, I suppose you won't mind helping for a bit till I see my way. What was the screw you got?

MARY Twenty-five.

JOHN That would help if the worst came to the worst.

MARY We lived on it before.

JOHN We could put up at the same lodgings for a bit. They're cheap.

MARY Walton Street.

JOHN *(loudly)* Anyway, I'm going to be even with him – I'll see him damned before I submit. I've put up with it long enough for your sake – I'm going to get a bit of my own back for once. After all, I'm his son – you can't count Dick; when I'm gone he'll begin to see what he's lost. Why, he may as well sell Rutherford's outright – with no one to come after him. He's worked for that – all his life! Lord! I'd give something to see his face when he comes in and asks for me!

MARY *makes no answer, as indeed there is none to make. She speaks again, not bitterly, but as one stating a fact.*

MARY So that's your plan. *(There is a silence, in which he cannot meet her eyes. She repeats, without hope)* John, once more – from my soul I ask you to do what I wish.

JOHN *(impatiently)* What about?

MARY The money. To put it back. *(He makes a movement of desperate irritation)* No, don't answer just for a moment. You don't know how much depends on this – for us both. Our future life – perhaps our last chance of happiness together you don't know what it may decide.

JOHN I tell you you don't understand. *(There is a blank silence. He moves uncomfortably)* You can't see. What's twenty-three quid!

She makes a despairing movement.

MARY *(in a changed voice)* I'm afraid you'll find it rather a burden having me and Tony – while you're seeing your way, I mean.

JOHN A burden? You? Why, you've just said you could help at Mason's—

MARY I can't go out all day and leave Tony.

JOHN Old Mrs What's-'er-name would keep an eye on him.

MARY It would free you a good deal if we weren't with you.

JOHN Of course if you won't do anything to help—

MARY *(after a pause)* How would it be if you went alone? Then – when you've seen your way – when you've made enough just to live decently – you could write and we could come to you. Somewhere that would do for Tony – wherever it may be.

JOHN In a month or two.

MARY In a month or two.

JOHN *(awkwardly)* Well, perhaps it would be better – as you suggest it. I really don't exactly see how I'm going to manage the two of you... You mean – stay on here in the meantime.

MARY Yes – stay on here.

JOHN But the Guv'nor – I'm afraid it'll be pretty rotten for you without me.

MARY That's all right.

JOHN *(irritably)* All these stupid little details – we lose sight of the real issue. That's settled, then.

MARY Yes – settled. *(She moves, passing her hand over her eyes)* How are you going?

JOHN *(relieved)* What's the time now? Close on twelve!

MARY You're not thinking of going now – at once!

JOHN There's the one o'clock train. I'll get old Smith to drive me to the Junction – it doesn't stop.

MARY There won't be time to pack your things.

JOHN Send them after me.

MARY You've no food to take with you.

JOHN That doesn't matter; I'll get some on the way.

MARY *(suddenly)* You can't go like this! We must talk – we can't end it all like this.

JOHN I must – I didn't know it was so late – he'll be in to dinner. Cheer up, dear, it's only for a little while. I hate it too, but it wouldn't do for him to find me here. It would look – weak.

MARY No, no – you're right – you mustn't meet – it would do no good. *(She stands undecided for a moment, then goes quickly into the hall and brings his overcoat)* It's bitter cold. And it's an open trap, isn't it?

JOHN I shall be all right. *(She helps him on with the coat)* It won't be long – the time'll pass before you know where you are; it always does – I haven't time to see the kid – it's the only thing to be done – other fellows make their fortunes every day, why shouldn't I?

MARY *(as if he were a child)* Yes, yes, why shouldn't you?

JOHN Something'll turn up – and I've got the devil's own luck at times – you'll see. I've never had a chance up to now. Some day you'll believe in me. *(He sees her face and stops short)* Mollie—! *(Takes her in his arms. She breaks down, clinging to him)*

MARY Oh, my dear – if I could!

JOHN *(moved)* I will do it, Mollie – I swear I will. Something'll turn up, and it'll all come right – we'll be as happy as kings, you see if we aren't. Don't, dear, it's only for a little while... Well then – will you come with me now?

MARY No, no, that can't be. Go, go – he'll be in directly. Go now.

She goes with him to the outer door. ANN RUTHERFORD *comes in on her way through the room.*

ANN Who is it's got the door open on such a day? And the wind fit to freeze a body's bones! *(The outer door is heard closing.* MARY *comes in slowly, very pale.)* Come in, come in, for the Lord's sake. *(Looking at her)* What be ye doing out there?

MARY He's gone.

ANN *(cross with the cold)* Gone, gone, this one and that – John? And what'll he be gone for? I never seed such doings, never!

MARY Shall I make up the fire?

ANN And you all been and let it down. Nay, nay, I'll do it myself. It'll not be up for ten minutes or more. Such doings. What'll he be gone for?

MARY He's had a quarrel with his father.

ANN *(putting logs on, half-whimpering)* A fine reason for making folks talk – bringing disgrace on the house, and all Grantley talking, and tomorrow Sunday – I never seed the like, never!

MARY It's no use crying.

ANN It's weel enough for you to talk – you bain't one of the family, a stranger like you. You don't know. When you've come up i' the world and are respected, there's nothing pleases folk better than to find something again you. What am I to say when I'm asked after my nevvy? Tell me that. And him gone off without so much as a change to his back – it aren't respectable. And there's Janet not ten minutes since gone along the road wi' her shawl over her head like a common working lass. Where it's to end, I'm sure I can't tell.

MARY Perhaps it is ended.

ANN Perhaps half the work's left and the house upset. Susan'll be giving notice just now – her and her goings on. As if lasses weren't hard enough to get – and there's dinner and all—

MARY Do you want the table laid?

ANN It'd help – though you've no call to do it – you got your own troubles – the little lad'll be wanting you mebbee.

MARY He's still asleep. I'll leave the door open and then I shall hear him. *(She opens the door, listening for a moment before she comes back into the room)*

ANN Janet'll be back mebbee afore you've finished. Such doings – everything put wrong. I'll go and fetch the bread. *(She wanders out, talking as she goes)*

MARY takes the red cloth off the table, folds it, takes the white one from the drawer in the sideboard, and spreads it. As she is doing so RUTHERFORD comes in. He stands looking at her for a moment, then comes to the fire.

RUTHERFORD *(as he passes her)* Dinner's late.

MARY *(going on with her work)* It'll be ready in a few minutes.

RUTHERFORD It's gone twelve.

She makes no answer. He takes his pipe off the chimney-piece and begins to fill it. As he is putting his tobacco-pouch back into his pocket his eye fall on the table; he stops short.

You've laid a place short. *(Raising his voice)* D'ye hear me, you've laid a—

She looks at him.

MARY No.

She goes to the sideboard and spreads a cloth there. He stands motionless staring at the table.

RUTHERFORD Gone. Trying to frighten me, is he? Trying a bit o' bluff – he'll show me, eh? And all I got to do is sit quiet and wait for him to come back – that's all I got to do.

MARY *(quietly)* He won't come back.

RUTHERFORD Won't he! He'll come back right enough when he feels the pinch – he'll come slinking back like a whipped puppy at nightfall, like he did afore. I know him – light – light-minded like his mother afore him. *(He comes to his desk and finds the* *open cash box)* Who's been here? Who's been here? *(He stands staring at the box till the lid falls from his hand)* Nay – he'll not come back, by God!

MARY *(hopelessly)* He thought he had the right – he believed he had the right after you'd taken what was his.

RUTHERFORD I'd sooner have seen him in his grave.

MARY He couldn't see.

RUTHERFORD Bill Henderson did that because he knowed no better. And my son knowed no better, though I made a gentleman of him. Set him up. I done with him – done with him.

He drops heavily into the arm-chair beside the table and sits staring before him. After a long silence he speaks again.

Why haven't you gone too, and made an empty house of it?

MARY I'm not going.

RUTHERFORD Not going, aren't you? Not till it pleases you, I take it – till he sends for you?

MARY He won't send for me.

RUTHERFORD *(quickly)* Where's the little lad?

MARY Asleep upstairs. *(After a pause she speaks again in level tones)* I've lived in your house for nearly three months. *(He turns to look at her)* Until you came in just now you haven't spoken to me half-a-dozen times. Every slight that can be done without words you've put upon me. There's never a day passed but you've made me feel that I'd no right here, no place.

RUTHERFORD You'll not die for a soft word from the likes o' me.

MARY Now that I've got to speak to you, I want to say that first – in case you should think I'm going to appeal to you and in case I should be tempted to do it.

RUTHERFORD What ha' ye got to ask of me?

MARY To ask – nothing. I've a bargain to make with you.

RUTHERFORD *(half truculent)* Wi' me?

MARY You can listen – then you can take it or leave it.

RUTHERFORD Thank ye kindly. And what's your idea of a bargain?

MARY A bargain is where one person has something to sell that another wants to buy. There's no love in it – only money – money that pays for life. I've got something to sell that you want to buy.

RUTHERFORD What's that?

MARY My son. *(Their eyes meet in a long steady look. She goes on deliberately)* You've lost everything you have in the world. John's gone – and Richard – and Janet. They won't come back. You're alone now and getting old, with no one to come after you. When you die Rutherford's will be sold – somebody'll buy it and give it a new name perhaps, and no one will even remember that you made it. That'll be the end of all your work. Just – nothing. You've thought of that. I've seen you thinking of it as I've sat by and watched you. And now it's come... Will you listen?

RUTHERFORD Ay.

She sits down at the other end of the table, facing him.

MARY It's for my boy. I want – a chance of life for him – his place in the world. John can't give him that, because he's made so. If I went to London and worked my hardest I'd get twenty-five shillings a week. We've failed. From you I can get what I want for my boy. I want – all the good common things: a good house, good food, warmth. He's a delicate little thing now, but he'll grow strong like other children. I want to undo the wrong we've done him, John and I. If I can. Later on there'll be his schooling – I could never save enough for that. You can give me all this – you've got the power. Right or wrong, you've got the power... That's the bargain. Give me what I ask, and in return I'll give you – him. On one condition. I'm to stay on here. I won't trouble you – you needn't speak to me or see me unless you want to. For ten years he's to be absolutely mine, to do what I like with. You mustn't interfere – you mustn't tell him to do things or frighten him. He's mine. For ten years more.

RUTHERFORD And after that?

MARY He'll be yours.

RUTHERFORD To train up. For Rutherford's? You'd trust your son to me?

MARY Yes.

RUTHERFORD After all? After Dick, that I've bullied till he's fool? John, that's wished me dead?

MARY In ten years you'll be an old man; you won't be able to make people afraid of you any more.

RUTHERFORD Ah! Because o' that? And because I have the power?

MARY Yes. And there'll be money for his clothes – and you'll leave the Works to him when you die.

There is silence. He sits motionless, looking at her.

RUTHERFORD You've got a fair notion of business – for a woman.

MARY I've earned my living. I know all that that teaches a woman.

RUTHERFORD It's taught you one thing – to have an eye to the main chance.

MARY You think I'm – bargaining for myself?

RUTHERFORD You get a bit out of it, don't you?

MARY What?

RUTHERFORD A roof over your head – the shelter of a good name – your keep – things not so easy to come by, my son's wife, wi' a husband that goes off and leaves you to live on his father's charity. *(There is a pause)*

MARY *(slowly)* There'll be a woman living in the house – year after year, with the fells closed round her. She'll sit and sew at the window and see the furnaces glare in the dark; lock up, and give you the keys at night—

RUTHERFORD You've got your bairn.

MARY Yes, I've got him! For ten years. *(They sit silent)* Is it a bargain?

RUTHERFORD Ay. *(She gets up with a movement of relief. As he speaks again she turns, facing him)* You think me a hard man. So I am. But I'm wondering if I could ha' stood up as you're standing and done what you've done.

MARY I love my child. That makes me hard.

RUTHERFORD I used to hope for my son once, like you do for yours now. When he was a bit of a lad I used to think o' the day when I'd take him round and show him what I had to hand on. I thought he'd come after me – glad o' what I'd done. I set my heart on that. And the end of it's just this – an empty house – we two strangers, driving our bargain here across the table.

MARY There's nothing else.

RUTHERFORD You think I've used him badly? You think I've done a dirty thing about this metal?

MARY It was his.

RUTHERFORD I've stolen it behind his back – and I'm going to make money out of it?

MARY I don't know – I don't know.

RUTHERFORD It'll come to your son.

MARY Yes.

RUTHERFORD Because I done that he'll have his chance, his place i' the world. What would ha' gone to the winds, scattered and useless, 'll be his. He'll come on, young and strong, when my work's done, and Rutherford's 'll stand up firm and safe out o' the fight and the bitterness – Rutherford's that his grandfather gave his life to build up.

MARY *(stopping him with a gesture)* Hush!

RUTHERFORD What is it? *(they both listen)* The little lad. He's waking!

MARY runs out. The room is very silent as **RUTHERFORD** *sits sunk in his chair, thinking.*

PROPERTY LIST

Knitting (p1)
Baby's cap (p1)
Silver basket (p2)
Pair of carpet slippers (p3)
Lamp (p4)
Loaf on a trencher (p4)
Cigarette (p12)
Newspaper (p15)
Tray – cups and saucers (p16)
Forks (p18)
Papers (p21)
Bunch of keys (p21)
Leather purse or bag (p21)
Cash-box (p22)
Pipe (p23)
Letters (p24)
Papers (p36)
Bedroom candlesticks (p38)
Whisky (p51)
Reading lamp (p52)
Coins (p70)
Cash box (p73)
Money (p73)
Overcoat (p77)
White tablecloth (p79)
Pipe (p79)
Tobacco-pouch (p79)

COSTUME

Ann Rutherford – black dress with a big flat brooch and a cap with lilac ribbons (p1)
Janet – dark dress of some warm material with white collar and cuffs (p2)
Richard Rutherford – regulation clergyman's clothes (p14)
Mrs Henderson – draggled skirt and shawl over her head (p42)
Janet – shawl (p62)

LIGHTING

The lamp is burning on the larger table (p38)

SOUND

A voice is heard outside and then the outer door opens (p20)
The sound of a stick being put into the umbrella stand (p20)
A series of slow heavy knocks on the outer door are heard, ending with a belated single one (p42)
Another knock (p42)
A knock is heard on the outer door (p51)
Janet...is heard putting the chain on the outer door (p57)

THIS IS NOT THE END

Visit samuelfrench.co.uk
and discover the best
theatre bookshop
on the internet

A vast range of plays
Acting and theatre books
Gifts

samuelfrench.co.uk
samuelfrenchltd
samuel french uk